Praise for 365 ways to succeed with ADHD

"*The ADHD Awareness Book Project* is a must-read for anyone affected by ADHD. The book contains a bit of wisdom for each day of the year, written by over 80 contributors with a wealth of experience. I give this excellent book my highest recommendation."

~Kate Kelly, MSN, SCAC co-author of *You Mean I'm Not Lazy, Stupid or Crazy?!* and *The ADDed Dimension*

"Whether you have ADHD or are supporting someone with ADHD there is something for everyone in *The ADHD Awareness Book Project.* This book is an excellent resource! There has been a need for this type of book for a long time. Now, it is finally here!!!"

~David Giwerc, Founder & President, ADD Coach Academy, author of *Permission to Proceed: The Keys to Creating a Life of Passion, Purpose and Possibility for Adults with ADHD*

"What an inspired idea! This brilliant book should be on the bedside table of every person with ADHD. *365 Days* will rock your world; it could change your life."

~Linda Roggli, author, *Confessions of an ADDiva: midlife in the non-linear lane*

"*The ADHD Awareness Book Project* provides valuable tips and strategies for living with ADHD. This unique book offers a fresh perspective on how to thrive with ADHD, incorporating the wisdom and creativity of experts from around the globe."

~Jodi Sleeper-Triplett, MCC, SCAC, coach, trainer and author of *Empowering Youth with ADHD.*

"Full of wit and wisdom! Brilliant best tips from some of the best in the field and short enough to be read and appreciated by even those with ADHD who hate to read. Love it!

~Michelle Novotni, Ph.D. ADHD Expert; Psychologist and ADHD coach and author of *What Does Everybody Else Know that I Don't.*

"Never doubt that a small group of thoughtful, committed people can change the world. Indeed it is the only thing that ever has."

~Margaret Mead

The ADHD Awareness Book Project

365 ways to succeed with ADHD

A FULL YEAR OF VALUABLE TIPS & STRATEGIES FROM THE WORLD'S BEST ADHD COACHES & EXPERTS

Edited by Laurie Dupar, PMHNP, RN, PCC

365 ways to succeed with ADHD

ISBN: 978-0-615-52214-2

Publisher: Laurie Dupar
Granite Bay, CA

Cover Design by LiveYourMessage.com

Content edits by WriteAssociate.com

More About the "ADHD Awareness Book Project"

The ADHD Awareness Book Project was guided by these goals: Provide people living with ADHD valuable strategies and tips to help them better succeed and increase the awareness of ADHD worldwide.

Too often, in the last nine years as an ADHD Coach, I've met with parents, students and newly-diagnosed adults struggling alone, not knowing that answers to their challenges were available. Many had never heard the term "ADHD". They had no idea that there were alternative ways to succeed by doing things that better fit with their ADHD brain style. Frankly, I am tired. I am tired of knowing that young children to adults in their 70's are struggling alone with ADHD, unaware that there are answers, resources, hope and help out here. I am not alone.

Last June, believing in the power of community and the dedication of my colleagues, I announced that I would be coordinating a book of tips and strategies for succeeding with ADHD, featuring as many ADHD experts as possible. I invited all the ADHD professionals I knew and asked them to invite ADHD professionals they knew to participate in this project. Over 80 co-authors from around the world and from a variety of professions and expertise answered the call and submitted their answers to the question: "What is the best tip or strategy you have to help someone with ADHD succeed?" *The ADHD Awareness Book Project: 365 ways to succeed with ADHD* is their responses. Each co-author has contributed submitted valuable tips and strategies to help people with ADHD succeed. Within these pages there is something for every reader, that one tip, strategy, resource or idea that will be the answer you are most needing in this moment.

How you are making a difference!

Whether this book is for you or for someone you care about, a portion of the proceeds from national bookseller sales of *The ADHD Awareness Book Project: 365 ways to succeed with ADHD*, will be used to support three international ADHD organizations:

- Children and Adults with Attention Deficit/Hyperactivity Disorder (CHADD)
- Attention Deficit Disorder Association (ADDA)
- ADHD Coaches Organization (ACO)

Thank you for helping us increase the awareness of ADHD! ~Laurie Dupar. Editor

How to Use this Book

This book is intended to be "ADD friendly." It is formatted to include a large variety of tips that are short, succinct, easy to read and immediately useable. There is a full year of tips (365 total) in order to give you lots of variety and choice, without the limitations of calendar dates. This unique format was recommended to me by one of my students, Nik, who told me that putting specific dates on a book for people with ADHD might not be helpful because each person may want to read it their own way. Some of you may want to put it by your bedside and read one tip a day...terrific! Some of you may sit down in one sitting and read all the tips...have fun! Still others, in your very wonderful ADHD style, may thumb through the book, starting wherever it catches your attention, reading from the middle to the end...the end to the middle...or read every other page! It is yours to decide. Enjoy in whatever manner your wonderful ADHD brain chooses!

Contact the co-authors

As you read and you find a particular tip or strategy especially useful, I encourage you to connect with the book's co-authors via the contact information they have provided. They are looking forward to hearing from you!

Share your own personal ADHD success tip

We want to hear from you! Tell us what this book has meant to you, let me in on your personal favorite ADHD strategy, or tell us about your success story! I would love to hear from you! Please email me at: Laurie@ADHDAwarnessBookProject.com.

I look forward to hearing from you!

~Laurie Dupar, Editor,
365 ways to succeed with ADHD

Contents

"Everybody is a genius. But, if you judge a fish by its ability to climb a tree, it'll spend its whole life believing that it is stupid." *Albert Einstein*

"Change of any sort, requires courage." *Anonymous*

"Aim for success, not perfection."
Dr. David M. Burns

"You will come to know the way to success only when you know your strengths" *Varun Saurya A*

If A equals success, then the formula is A equals X plus Y and Z, with X being work, Y play and Z keeping your mouth shut." *Albert Einstein*

"The fastest way to succeed is to look as if you're playing by somebody else's rules, while quietly playing by your own." *Michael Konda*

"It is never too late to become who you might have been." *George Eliot*

"The secret to productive goal setting is establishing clearly defined goals, writing them down and then focusing on them several times a day with words and emotions as if we've already achieved them."
Denis Waitley

"Climb the stairway to the stars one step at a time."
Anonymous

The truly creative individual stands ready to abandon old habits and to acknowledge that life, particularly his own unique life, is rich with possibilities." *Frank Baron*

"We must be willing to get rid of the life we've planned, so as to have the life that is waiting for us."
Joseph Campbell

"Success is going from failure to failure without losing your enthusiasm." *Abraham Lincoln*

"Don't let what you cannot do interfere with what you can do." *John Wooden*

"If you run into a wall, don't turn around and give up. Figure out how to climb it, go through it, or work around it." *Michael Jordan*

"The important thing is not being afraid to take a chance. Remember, the greatest failure is to not try."
Debbie Fields

"The jump is so frightening between where I am and where I want to be. Because of all I may become, I will close my eyes and leap."
Mary Anne Radmacher

"Our greatest weakness lies in giving up. The most certain way to succeed is always to try just one more time." *Thomas A. Edison*

Dedication

This book is dedicated to people living with ADHD, wherever you are. Your commitment, perseverance and determination for answers about how to live successfully with ADHD are a constant source of inspiration. YOU are the experts. YOU are the source for what we know "works" and what, even though it might make sense, doesn't.

It is also dedicated to ADHD professionals who are committed to making a positive difference in the lives of people with ADHD. These experts include: doctors, therapists, nutritional experts, coaches, educators, lawyers, accountants, organizational specialists and many more. Many of you chose to share your expertise by being a co-author in this book. Thank you all. I am proud to be your colleague.

Individually, we make a difference in the lives of people with ADHD. Together, there is the bigger possibility to positively change the world's understanding and awareness of ADHD. This book could not have happened without ALL of you.

Thank you

Acknowledgements

Putting this book together, was a labor of love borne by a passion, to make a positive difference in the lives of people with ADHD.

In fact, I can say it was with an "ADD-spirit" that this book was written and published. I had an idea, and I was determined to make it a reality without thought to the obstacles, road blocks, naysayers or disbelievers. Foremost in my thoughts was you, the people I had met and had yet to meet who had ADHD. Always on my mind I knew that this is what someone with ADHD would do. You would find a way through the obstacles, keep your eye on the goal despite the impossibility and get up each day determined and hopeful to succeed. You were the inspiration. Thank you.

I also want to thank all of the co-authors of *The ADHD Awareness Book Project: 365 ways to succeed with ADHD.* Your individual and collective belief, support and contributions to this book have made it a reality. I am humbled by your generosity. And of course I want to thank my family, you know who you are; without your constant belief in me and undying patience, this would not have been possible. I love you all.

I also want to thank my assistant, Deanna McAdams, whose expertise and experience helped guide the way toward this publication. The staff at LiveYourMessage.com who created the book cover and Tammi Metzler at TheWriteAssociate.com, whose expertise and craft with words helped us all "sparkle." This wouldn't have been possible without all of you.

Thank you!

~Laurie Dupar

Introduction

Thirteen years ago, my youngest son was diagnosed with ADHD. As a mental health professional, used to having the answers, I uncharacteristically found myself searching for something that would help me better understand this mental health disorder and help him better manage his challenges. At the time, resources were scarce. Several years later, I discovered ADHD coaching and saw how much of a difference this approach made in helping both of us minimize our struggles and experience success. Surprising even myself, I have been an ADHD coach for the past nine years, and my son has pursued his dream and is serving in the United States Navy.

I never set out to be an ADHD coach. Having earned my Master's degree as a Psychiatric Mental Health Nurse Practitioner, I was prepared to diagnose and treat the whole array of mental health disorders. I would have never believed that understanding, advocating or focusing on working with people diagnosed with ADHD would have been so life-consuming and rewarding. Instead, I have been amazed with the consistent and never-slowing stream of people challenged with this disorder. As an ADHD coach, I get to work with some of the most amazingly brilliant and creative people everyday...and these are just my clients. The experts, professionals and specialists who focus on working with people diagnosed with ADHD are equally as incredible.

ADHD is a 24/7 disorder affecting people's ability to focus, pay attention, plan, prioritize and a whole host of other challenges. For some people with ADHD it is difficult to do less interesting tasks, like homework, bills, organizing or planning. The inability to complete these tasks has created huge disorder and chaos in their lives. For others, they struggle with finding motivation or fighting distractions from an inner sense of restlessness throughout the day from the moment they wake up to the hours they are trying to fall asleep. That's the thing about ADHD...it is so different for everyone.

There are some amazing international organizations available for people to better understand ADHD. I encourage you to seek out the resources from such organizations as Children and Adults with Attention Deficit Disorder (CHADD), www.chadd.org; Adults with Attention Deficit Disorder Association (ADDA), www.add.org; and the ADHD Coaches Organization (ACO), www.adhdcoaches.org.

In addition, there are many books written by authors who really understand the challenges of ADHD, many of whom have contributed to this book. I encourage you to explore their wisdom. I believe we can never know too much about ADHD.

And last but not least, there are the individual professionals who serve the ADHD community. Coaches, doctors, researchers, therapists, nutritionists, educators, lawyers, etc. Over the years, I have been awed at this community's dedication and commitment to serve each in their own way, using their unique strengths, talents and gifts to improve the lives of people with ADHD.

This book was an opportunity for all of these people and resources to come together in one place and share their "gems" with you. It is written with parents, families, children, teachers, teens, college students and adults of all ages in mind. There is literally something for everyone! Drawing from their wide variety of expertise and experience, these experts have offered you their best strategies and tips to help you succeed with ADHD. I know you will enjoy and find value in all of their contributions.

"Everybody is a genius. But, if you judge a fish by its ability to climb a tree, it'll spend its whole life believing that it is stupid."

~Albert Einstein

Hitting Roadblocks

When you hit a wall, it makes sense to stop instead of trying to push your way through it. If you have trouble or become overwhelmed, paralyzed or feel like you are running in circles, stop doing whatever it is and take a break. Learn how to operate your brain expertly. Know under which circumstances it works well and when it has to struggle too much. Get to know when it needs more stimulation, less stress, more nourishment or structure or support, and when it is stretched too thin or wound too tight. Then, give it what it needs.

~Sari Solden, Author

Sari Solden, a psychotherapist in Ann Arbor, MI, has worked with adults with ADHD for 23 years and is a national speaker and the author of *Women with ADD* and *Journeys Through ADDulthood.* ADDJourneys.com sari@sarisolden.com

Is Your ADHD Child Always at Fault?

Many parents believe that they should punish their child when they misbehave at school.

It has been shown that punishment is not an effective way to change a behavior or get a child to do what you want, especially in children with ADHD. When a child misbehaves, natural and/or logical consequences are the best way to address the problem and to investigate the behavior to understand what precipitated your child's behavior. In school, many children with ADHD have impulsive or poorly-thought-out reactions to negative events, such as doing poorly on a test, being hurried, being bullied, teased, or provoked.

~Roya Kravetz, ADHD Coach

Roya Kravetz, Credentialed Life Coach, ADHD Coach and Consultant, and Parent Educator. Specializes in ADHD Coaching and/or related challenges roya@adhdsuccesscoaching.com

Increase Awareness of Social Skills

Difficulty with social skills is common in students with ADHD and related challenges. The use of a camcorder can help students recognize how their actions might be perceived by others. One can shoot a video of an actual encounter with the permission of all parties or have the students practice certain skills in a made-up scenario. After the students watch the video, they can discuss what was noticed and what skills might be worked on. The students might enjoy watching a before and after video to appreciate the progress in these important skills.

For more information, go to:
www.FocusForEffectiveness.com/blog.

~Roxanne Fouche, ADHD Caoch

Roxanne Fouche, ADHD Coach and Consultant, specializes in working with individuals of all ages with ADHD/LD and relatedchallenges.
Roxanne@FocusForEffectiveness.com
(858) 484-4749

Take Time to Play

One of the biggest challenges for my clients is taking "time off" seriously. The cost/benefit of not taking breaks from today's busy life only sets one up for more burnout and loss of control. Fun must be scheduled into your life! Hire a travel agent to book annual vacations, set weekly "date nights" with your partner, create a ritual of meeting friends weekly for dinner. Tap into your creative side by taking a cooking or dance class. The point is to do what you love without guilt. Life is too short!

Fun and play are essential for rejuvenation.

~Nancy A Ratey, Ed.M., MCC

Nancy A. Ratey, Ed.M., MCC, is a Strategic Life Coach specializing in coaching professionals with ADHD. She is the author of *The Disorganized Mind,* www.NancyRatey.com

Are you ADHD?

Parenting a child with ADHD can be a 24/7 extreme rollercoaster ride. Parents of an ADHD child can enjoy the highest highs and the lowest lows. Providing a level playing field, establishing consistency and maintaining calm can be some of our best tools in getting through these years. If you are a parent with ADHD, these strategies might not be so easy. If you have ADHD yourself, recognize that at times your own struggles may be intensified by your child's and visa versa. Seek out people you trust to support you. Find a support group for people with ADHD nearby, or start one yourself. Most of all, know that recognizing and understanding your own ADHD is the first step to both your and your child's success.

~Laurie Dupar, PMHNP, RN, PCC

Laurie Dupar, PMHNP, Certified ADHD Coach, specializes in helping you understand your brain, navigate the treatment maze, reduce your challenges and get things done! www.CoachingforADHD.com

Rotate Protein to Boost Brain Power

Eating the same proteins is boring. Our body also becomes bored and used to amino acids in that food, making it difficult to create new strains of amino acids, thus diminishing neurotransmitter availability and decreasing focus. Making changes in protein increases your availability to create new strains and improve brain power. Try fish or tofu instead of chicken on your salad. Add protein powder to your morning oatmeal instead of just milk; try hummus and pita chips instead of potato chips or almond butter instead of your classic PB&J. Food is the fuel to keep you focused.

~Emily Roberts, MA, LPC

Emily Roberts, MA, LPC, is a psychotherapist who works with Neurogistics and helps parents balance their child's brain naturally. www.Neurogistics.com

Let 'em Bake!

Teenagers and young adults have a chronological age, an intellectual age, and a social maturity age. These three are rarely the same. With ADHD teens, often the intellectual age is years ahead of the chronological age, with the social maturity age three to five years, or more, behind the chronological age. Lots of patience is required of parents, as maturity comes later for these teens. The greatest gift parents can give their ADHD teens is unconditional love and patience. It takes longer for these delightful and creative folks to reach a balanced level of social maturity.

~Dee Shofner Doochin, MLAS

Dee Doochin, MLAS, Professional Certified Coach, Certified Mentor Coach, Senior Certified ADHD Coach, wife, mother, grandmother, great-grandmother with ADHD, adventurer, lover of life! www.addupcoach.com

Spend A Little Time Planning

A morning routine, a grocery trip, and a vacation all require many steps. Planning just requires you to spend some time figuring them out. So sit down and think about the parts of the project or job. Write them down. Figure out the best order. Test the plan. If it works, good. Do it again. If it doesn't, figure out what went wrong and revise the plan. Find a system that works for you and use it... no matter what your mother or someone else says.

~Kerch McConlogue, PCC, CPCC

Kerch McConlogue, PCC, CPCC, works with adults in Baltimore and around the world who have ADHD. Find her on the web at: www.mapthefuture.com

Be Connected with Your Children

If you wish to become more aware of your children's needs, be there. Parents who share a secure relationship with their children are better at reading their children's cues and respond better to their children's needs. Use these tips:

1. Be consistent. Do as you say and say as you do.
2. Be attuned to individual needs. Listen, watch and respond.
3. Proximity matters. Respond to them by getting off the phone and off the couch.
4. Acknowledge their feelings and take your children seriously.
5. When your child is excited, be equally excited and share the happiness.
6. When your children need you, give them your undivided attention.

A secure relationship will help you and your children build a happy relationship. Enjoy.

~Lynne Kenney, PsyD

Lynne Kenney, PsyD. is a mom, pediatric psychologist and author of *The Family Coach Method* (St. Lynn's Press). www.lynnekenney.com

Controlling Chaos in the Classroom

Teachers know the disruption students with ADHD can bring to their classroom by blurting out answers or speaking out of turn. The issue stems from their poor working memory and impulsivity. They are afraid they will forget the answer so they yell it out as soon as it comes to them.

Instead of scolding them, try this: Ask them to raise their hand and at the same time write the answer down. Now they are confident they won't forget it. This will mitigate their impulsivity to yell out.

Physically recognize their good behavior with a pat on the shoulder or thumbs up.

~Dr. Billi, Ph.D.

The AttentionB Method, Pedagogical/Class Management for ADHD, www.AttentionB.com (855) DrBilli

Create a Permanent Grocery List

Go through your cabinets, refrigerator, pantry and freezer and make a list of the things you replace most often. Then type up the list in the computer and add checkbox beside each item. If you are really organized, sort the items in the order of your favorite grocery store aisles. Print out the list and post it on the refrigerator. When you run out of something, simply check off that item. Don't forget to take the list to the store!

~Linda Roggli PCC, CLC

Linda Roggli, PCC, CLC Professional Certified Coach, Author of *"Confessions of an ADDiva: midlife in the non-linear lane"* http://confessionsofanaddiva.net

What are You Hiding in Your Closet?

Although I'd be willing to bet that you've got a few surprises in there from your last stash-and-dash cleanup, I'd also bet there's something lurking in there that's so insidious that it keeps you from reaching your potential and feeling fulfilled. I'm talking about perfectionism. Often, we allow our need to do things "the right way" to keep us from doing things at all. Next time you're struggling to follow through on something, ask yourself whether you're focusing on doing it "right," or doing it "well enough." This perspective shift might actually help you clean out that closet—for good!

~Lynne Edris

Lynne Edris is a woman with ADD, Mom to an ADHD Teen, and a professional ADD Coach. "My life is like the ADD channel: All ADD, All the Time!"

Pennies in Your Pocket

Do you feel like you're in the rut of always pointing out what's wrong with an ADHD child?

This game helps to break the cycle.

Start with five pennies in your pocket. Every time you notice something good with the child, point it out.

Move the penny from one pocket to another.

The goal is to get your pennies in the other pocket.

The next day, increase momentum by adding more pennies or larger coins for something really big.

Soon, your child will respond to the positive feedback and begin shifting towards better behavior and self-esteem.

~Robin Nordmeyer

Robin Nordmeyer on ADHD, www.LifeAheadCoaching.com

When Ashamed, Act "As If"

If you suffer from shame every time you "screw up" and your shame makes you avoid dealing with the problem, you are probably making consequences worse. Next time you feel ashamed of something you did, said or missed doing, think of what a self-confident person would do. They might laugh at themselves, make light of it, apologize or simply own up to the mistake and move on. Practice acting AS IF you were confident and can take mistakes in stride. It will improve other people's perceptions of you, and you will behave more functionally instead of being paralyzed by shame.

~Bonnie Mincu

Bonnie Mincu, Senior ADHD Coach and founder of "THRIVE with ADD," has numerous classes, tools and resources on Adult ADHD challenges at:: www.thrivewithadd.com bonnie@bonniemincu.com (914) 478-0071

Beyond Simply ADHD

The key behavioral characteristics often thought of with ADHD are hyperactivity, impulsivity and distraction. In everyday life, however, children with ADHD have a much longer list of challenges, including:

- Emotional immaturity
- Difficulty in learning to read, write, or spell
- Poor handwriting
- Doing homework but forgetting to turn it in
- Difficulty changing routines
- Prone to accidents
- Excessive fidgets
- Seems easily frustrated
- May be demanding and difficult to please
- Is messy, disorganized and chaotic

If you think your child might have ADHD, knowing is the first step…learning more about ADHD is the answer.

~Laurie Dupar, PMHNP, RN, PCC

Laurie Dupar, Nurse Practitioner & ADHD Coach, specializes in helping you understand your brain, navigate the treatment maze, reduce challenges and get things done! www.CoachingforADHD.com

Advocacy Begins at Home

Too many parents feel the need to protect their children from social stigmas and keep ADHD a secret. But while their motives are noble, they are actually perpetuating the stigmas that they are trying to protect their children from. Unfortunately, secrecy breeds shame and magnifies an already poor sense of self esteem. Furthermore, it leaves many students unable to advocate for themselves when they move on to college. Include your child in the advocacy process. It can be tremendously empowering for them. Stress the fact that they have talents that are to be encouraged and challenges that they must respect and learn to navigate. But most of all, enjoy them for who they are. They are not broken, just different.

~Robert M. Tudisco, Esq.

Robert M. Tudisco, Esq., attorney, writer, ADHD adult and Executive Director of the Edge Foundation, a nonprofit specializing in coaching support for students with ADHD. www.edgefoundation.org

Change the Time to Be on Time!

Adults with ADD / ADHD often have challenges when it comes to being on time for appointments. One strategy that my ADHD coaching clients often find helpful is to think about the time they need to leave for the appointment instead of the appointment time itself. Get into the habit of putting the time you need to leave in your calendar and setting reminders and alarms for this time. Also practice training your mind to think of the time to leave instead of the actual appointment time. Keep practicing this again and again until it becomes a natural way of thinking.

~Tara McGillicuddy, SCAC

Tara McGillicuddy is a Senior Certified ADHD Coach and internationally-recognized ADHD Expert. Learn more about Tara and her ADHD resources at www.youraddcoach.com

The Trapper Keeper Phase

Starting a new relationship is like the first day of school. Everything feels different. Ordinary school supplies seem magical and hold the promise of something amazing.

ADHDers often only see this part, the promise of something amazing. Then, as shiny pencils lose their magic doing math and the TrapperKeeper breaks its promise of effortless organization, you start wondering why all of your school supplies are blue when you like green best.

To get through this "TrapperKeeper" phase, allow yourself to enjoy the shiny possibilities without losing sight of the fact that green is really your favorite color.

~Rori Boyce, ADHD Coach

Rori Boyce, ADHD Coach, Turning Leaf Life Coaching, Alton Bay, NH
www.turningleafcoaching.com

Best Money Management Tools

If you have trouble keeping on top of your financial situation and are comfortable with online banking, try Mint.com or PageOnce.com. Just create an account (don't forget to write down your login ID and password in a secure place!), plug in your login information for your bank account, credit cards, phone bill, etc., and watch these tools keep track of your income and bills. All of your financial info will be in one place, with charts showing you where your money goes, easy-to-use budgeting tools, and advice on how to better manage your money. It doesn't get easier.

~Sarah D. Wright M.S., A.C.T.

Sarah D. Wright, M.S., A.C.T., internationally-known ADHD coach, speaker, author, expert, and founding Board Member of the ADHD Coaches Organization. Sarah@FocusForEffectiveness.com

Sustainable Motivation

Parents often ask, "How can I motivate my child?" My answer: true, sustainable motivation comes from within – it is intrinsic. It develops as we support our children's need for emotional connection, autonomy, self-determination, and a feeling of competence.

What role do external consequences play in motivating children? Once you AND your child truly understand each other's perspective of the issues and problems…AND your child is aware of what the potential positive AND negative consequences are (natural and otherwise)…AND you know that your child is response-ABLE, then external consequences can help build skills, consistency and accountability.

~Cindy Goldrich, Ed. M., ACAC

Cindy Goldrich, Ed. M., ACAC, Certified ADHD Parent Coach
www.PTScoaching.com Cindy@PTScoaching.com
(516) 802-0593
Coaching available in New York and Telephone.
Parent the Child YOU have!

"Change of any sort requires courage"

~Anonymous

Isn't That Fascinating?

When something doesn't go well for your child, like a failed test, try what Benjamin Zander (educator and conductor) does instead of the typical negative response. With a smile on your face, delight in your voice and arms raised in the air, say, "Isn't that fascinating?" Then, while they are looking at you like you are nuts, say, "You just learned one way not to pass a math test. I wonder what would work better?" Cultivating a spirit of curiosity and possibilities will help avoid negative downward spiral thinking. Try it; you will be amazed at the results.

~Cindy Lea, MA

Cindy Lea, MA, Psychotherapist, ADD Coach & Speaker. Inspiring others by focusing on possibilities with warmth & humor. Minneapolis, MN www.SucceedingWithADD.com, Cindy@succeedingwithadd.com (612) 965-3052

Lessons from the "Tortoise and the Hare"

Although the hare could outrun the tortoise, he failed because after a strong start, he lost his focus, got distracted, forgot what he was doing, and took a nap.

The tortoise, although slow and steady—i.e. strong on persistence—won the race. Sound familiar?

How often do you put off - or fail to finish - lengthy, tedious tasks?

Next time, try time sprints! The intensity of racing will increase your focus. When overwhelmed by a large assignment, break it into several small tasks. For each task, sprint against time. Mark you goal, set your timer, and go for the win!

~Roland Rotz, Ph.d.

Roland Rotz, Ph.D. and Coach Sarah D. Wright, M.S., A.C.T., internationally-known authors, speakers, and ADHD experts. www.FidgetToFocus.com

Advice to Parents as an Advocate, Mother and Teacher!

Your child will need assistance! The steps? Start early! Get an official diagnosis. Do research; *LD Online* is a great place to begin. Inform the school. Get assistance. Choose an IEP or a 504 plan. Both help "level the playing field." Get out of the mix; hire a Coach or Advocate. Stay connected with weekly e-mails about assignments, tests and grades. Keep copies! Stay current! Don't assume teachers or principals know about ADHD, or will offer to help. Your children will learn to advocate for themselves from you! Accommodations help your children learn the curriculum their way. It is not cheating.

~Sandy Alletto Corbin, M.A.

Ms. Sandy Alletto Corbin, M.A., SCAC, Certified Senior ADHD Coach and Advocate working with families, teens and women. She can be reached at www.lifecoachsandyalletto.com

Avoid the Overwhelm Meltdown

People with ADHD often have tons of ideas and begin many projects, but have difficulty getting things done. This buildup of unfinished tasks contributes to confusion and anxiety, which can lead to zoning out (surfing the internet, TV, computer games, sleeping, etc).

There are many strategies to prevent overwhelm, but my favorite is to 'think small.' The idea is to get in action by starting on something... anything.

When feeling functional, prioritize projects and divide them into tasks. Now, pick any task to work on for just 10 minutes. That's often enough to pull you out of inertia.

~Susan Karyn Lasky, M.A., SCAC

Susan Lasky is a Master ADHD Strategist, Productivity & Organization Coach, helping adults and older students to get things done and enjoy life! Susan@SusanLasky.com (914) 373-4787

Teachers' Secret Power Punch

Without investing any extra time, teachers can reinforce easy ways to stay organized. What's the secret? Hole-punched paper!

Imagine if every handout, worksheet, quiz or test was printed on hole-punched paper. When students were given a handout, they could put it in their binder behind the tab marked "Handouts." When tests are returned, it would take 15 seconds to file work behind the "Tests & Quizzes" tab. This single daily action could lead to binders free of loose papers,students who can find things and a new habit.

What an easy way to teach that "clutter really does happen when we fail to make a decision."

~Becky Wheeler, ADHD Coach

Rebecca C. Wheeler, ADHD & Life Coach, New Focus Coaching, LLC, Alexandria, VA Structure Skills Strategy Support.
bwheeler@newfocuscoach.com (703) 980-0809

Popsicle Stick Chores

Doing daily chores can often become a boring task for children with ADHD. Boring = not getting done! To help make it a bit more exciting, I will write each chore on a popsicle stick and put it in a "what's next?" jar. Each morning, my children would be eager to see which "chore" they would be doing next based on what stick they pulled. As each stick was pulled and chore completed, they would mark it off until all were done! Sticks went back into a special "done" cup to get ready for tomorrow.

~Laurie Dupar, PMHNP, RN, PCC

Laurie Dupar, Certified ADHD Coach, specializes in helping you understand your brain, navigate the treatment maze, reduce your challenges and get things done! www.CoachingforADHD.com

"Growing" Through Life

1. Develop connections (friends, spiritual, etc.).
2. Self advocate. Ask for help.
3. Structure + balance + flexibility = :)!
4. Reward yourself. Don't wait until perfect!
5. Notice what you feel and your response. Don't judge the emotion.
6. "Chunk down": divide every job into workable chunks.
7. Find and explore your strengths! We know our weaknesses!
8. Listen to your body and trust it. Let go of the negative self-talk.
9. Be always at choice. You can always begin again!
10. Find what works for you. No need to do things as others do!
11. Sometimes letting yourseld just "do it" will allow you to run!
12. Smile and breathe!

~Ana Isabel Sánchez, Certified Coach

Mom. Wife. Attorney. Certified Coach with ADHD Training. Passion: Helping others take ownership of their lives and focus on their strengths to reach success.

Forget My Kid! How Do I Survive High School?

Parenting an ADHD teen in high school can be very stressful! Immature social skills, impulsivity and the need to be organized can create frustration for everyone. Here's some tips for parents:

- Call a teacher meeting three weeks into the school year to discuss your teen's challenges/academic needs.
- Provide all contact information so teachers can reach you easily.
- Ask for a set of textbooks for home use.
- Request support services or accommodations that will assist your teen academically.
- Be proactive...contact teachers intermittently for progress report.
- Enroll your teen into an activity that promotes self-esteem, like sports, band, student government.
- Give your teen a day off every now and then!

~Lisa-Anne Ray-Byers

Speech-Language Pathologist, Author and Columnist www.AskLisaAnne.com

Ozzie and Harriet and Family Dinners

Ok. So maybe we don't need Ozzie and Harriet, but our modern-day families need family dinners. Family dinners help us model organization and planning. Take 20 minutes, turn off your cell, TV, and radio, and tune into your kids/family/partner. Boil some pasta, cut a few veggies and tune out the busy world.

Focus on the positive and ask everyone what the best part of their day was. Try a family dinner night and see how simple it is to nurture your home nutritionally, emotionally, and spiritually.

~Hazel S.Kassel-Brief MSW, PCC

Hazel Brief, MSW, PCC www.SynergetiCoaching.com

Parenting with Rhythm

"Time to get up," says a mother lovingly.

"No!!!" screams her 5-year-old child. Sound familiar?

Getting my daughter ready for school was an everyday battle that stressed us both out. Instead of changing her habits, I changed mine. Because she had trouble waking, I'd bathe her at night, dress her in comfortable clothes for the next day and pack her toothbrush in her bag. When it was time to leave, I'd simply carry her to the car. She'd sleep all the way to school. By going with her rhythm instead of against it, we had peaceful mornings from then on.

~Dr. Billi, Ph.D.

The AttentionB Method, Parenting for ADHD www.AttentionB.com
(855) DrBilli

7 Tips for Taming ADHD Hypersensitivities

Most people with ADHD have at least some sensory hypersensitivity and may react to certain sounds, smells, fabrics, and more. Here are some tips to help you or your child:

1. Arrive to work early or stay late to avoid noise/interruptions from co-workers.
2. Find seamless socks, tagless shirts, and natural fabrics.
3. Allow your child to wear headphones during school lunch.
4. Add carpeting or throw rugs to cut down on house noise.
5. Use perfume-free products only.
6. Find a place to retreat to when overwhelmed – no matter where you go.
7. Use a small fan to block out noise.

~Terry Matlen, MSW, ACSW

Terry Matlen, ACSW, a nationally-recognized authority specializing in women with ADHD, is the author of *"Survival Tips for Women with ADHD"* and founder of www.ADDconsults.com

Seeing Is Achieving: 5 Tips for Visual Learners

Visual learners learn best by seeing information. These tips can help you take advantage of your unique learning style:

Tip # 1: Take and review notes. Include lots of details. Illustrate your notes.

Tip # 2: Create charts, graphs and mind maps of information you need to learn.

Tip # 3: Create and use your own flash cards. Review them often.

Tip # 4: Find a place to study that is the least distracting for you.

Tip # 5: Keep the "big picture" in mind and in front of you when studying the details of a subject.

~Laurie Moore Skillings, SCAC

Laurie Moore Skillings, Senior Certified ADHD Coach, specializes in working with teens that have a hard time with school. Laurie can be reached at: laurie@addwithease.com

Stop Whining and Get to the Point

Your boss returned your job review with some inaccurate statements. You're very concerned and immediately want to go straight to his office and complain about what he wrote, tell him why the statement is wrong and get him to correct it NOW. Instead, stop the impulsive action! Wait 24 hours and when you speak to your boss, remember this acronym: FED - stick to the Facts, cut the Emotions, and no Defensive language. Paying attention to this acronym keeps the focus on the facts instead of your emotions or any defensive demeanor you may present, and the result is greater integrity.

~Joyce Kubik, ADHD Coach

Joyce Kubik, Author, Presenter, Researcher, and ADHD Coach & Skills Trainer, coaches adults, college students and is a coach trainer. Avon Lake, Ohio

Get Out of the House on Time!

Arriving on time to appointments can be challenging, especially for those with ADHD. To help, one might:

- Make a habit of putting keys, cell phones, glasses, etc., in a designated place so they can be easily found when you need to leave.
- Have a "launch pad" where you consistently put other things you need to take with you (e.g., backpack, dry cleaning, shopping list, etc.).
- Estimate commute time and then add time for unexpected events.
- Reward yourself for arriving early by having something fun to do as you wait (e.g., a magazine or book you've wanted to read, etc.)

~Roxanne Fouche, ADHD Coach

Roxanne Fouche, ADHD Coach and Consultant, specializes in working with individuals of all ages with ADHD/LD and related challenges. Roxanne@FocusForEffectiveness.com (858) 484-4749

Exercise is the Best Medicine

When I tell people I have a "medicine" that is proven to help ADHD symptoms, improve IQ, improve mood, prevent depression, and prevent a host of other health problems all with no cost and minimal side effects, they are very excited. That "medicine" is exercise. When my kids struggle with getting their homework done, I immediately prescribe 100 jumping jacks or a quick game of tag, and amazingly their concentration and focus magically improves. Commit to at least 10 minutes of brisk exercise per day and try a power walk before class or walking meetings.

~Dr. Susan Wilder

Dr. Susan Wilder, CEO of LifeScape Medical Associates and LifeScape Premier, is an expert in nutritional testing and interventions for mood/attention problems in adults and children. www.lifescapepremier.com (480) 860-5269

Mom's Time Out

As the mother of four, two with ADHD, life was often frustrating. Once, when family friends were touring our new home, my oldest son pointed to the laundry room and explained, "This is where my mom takes her time outs." At the time, I wasn't too pleased that he was airing my "dirty laundry," but now, years later, I realize that parenting ADHD children is unquestionably difficult for all of us on occasion. That taking a break from the overwhelm we sometimes feel building inside is healthy. Taking a time out allowed me to calm down before I said something or did something I would regret. Where is your "time out" spot?

~Laurie Dupar, PMHNP, RN, PCC

Laurie Dupar, PMHNP, Certified ADHD Coach, specializes in helping you understand your brain, navigate the treatment maze, reduce your challenges and get things done! www.CoachingforADHD.com

Saying Grace to Save Face

Let's face it, some people with AD(H)D tend to be a bit clumsy, forgetful, and, dare I say it, accident prone.

Rather than getting embarrassed or upset, one family's answer to potentially embarrassing situations is to make light of them by saying "Way to go, Grace" to the first 'Grace' to spill at a meal (trip, bump into something...)

Each family member, ADD or not, has been crowned 'Grace.' They laugh together and everyone's self-esteem is saved! Now, the kids understand that accidents happen, and it's ok. They even yell out 'Grace' before someone else can call them on it!

~Kricket Harrison, Professional Coach

Kricket Harrison, Professional Coach and Motivational Speaker, is an expert at maximizing creative potential and developing strategies for success based on individual learning styles. www.BrightOutsidetheBox.com

Utilize Financial Software

If you own a business, knowing your financial status is critical to the decision-making process. However, updating and entering transactions is tedious and can overwhelm us. Using financial software, such as QuickBooks, is a great strategy. Most products save transactions as you go and are user-friendly. You can enter one or two receipts or a boxful at a time. Today's financial software products are also portable and easy to send to an accountant or bookkeeper to update for you. The software is pretty universal, so it's easy to find someone who knows how to use it to help you.

~Karen Peak, CPA

Karen Peak - not your typical certified public accountant - runs a successful tax and bookkeeping practice in Northern California, helping entrepreneurial clients from coast to coast. www.karenpeakcpa.com

The Five-Minute Miracle

One of my clients found that he needed to have some tasks that gave him immediate success and a feeling of reward.

What he did was to create a 3-column paper and list tasks that can be completed in 5 minutes in one column, tasks that can be completed in 30 minutes in another column and tasks over 30 minutes in a third column.

That way, whenever he needed a success and a boost, he could choose a 5-minute task.

It also helped in filling in different open time slots he had in his calendar.

~Deb Bollom, PCC, PC-ACG, CPCC

Deb Bollom, PCC, PC-ACG, CPCC, works with ADHD entrepreneurs/adults who hate details, feel overwhelmed and want to move themselves and their businesses forward. www.d5coaching.com (715) 386-6860

The Power of ADHD Group Coaching

A mother with an adopted child was referred to me for a parent coaching group. Overwhelmed by her daughter's unruly behavior, this mother was left feeling as though returning her child to her country of origin was her only option.

Thanks to the supportive group environment of sharing emotions, thoughts, and experiences, this mother garnered considerable emotional support and practical advice. She also gained the crucial understanding of what ADHD was, how it affected her daughter, and the critical role that parents play in assisting their children to overcome challenges.

~Roya Kravetz, ADHD Coach

Roya Kravetz specializes in coaching youth and adults with ADHD, as well as educating and coaching parents regarding ADHD and/or related (858) 334-8584 challenges roya@focusforeffectiveness.com

Prepare ADHD Children for Social Gatherings

1. Children do best when prepared. Discuss in advance where you will be going and who will be there.
2. Practice together ways to greet adults and/or engage in table manners. Be realistic; expectations should be in line with your child's current ability to socialize and maintain impulse control.
3. Ask your child about his/her worries. It's important they know that they matter too.
4. Brainstorm together ways to stay occupied when bored.
5. Avoid disciplining in public. If a problem arises, find a private place to talk. Ask questions and problem solve instead of disciplining whenever possible.

~Linda Richmand, Life Coach

Linda Richmand, Business, Career, and Life Coach specializing in adult AD/H/D. www.CoachRichmand.com (914) 330-9103

Think Your Child Has ADHD?

What to do now? Six steps to get your child the support they deserve:

1. Establish a good relationship with your child's teacher, meeting with them to find out if they have any concerns.
2. Learn about ADHD at www.chadd.org.
3. Schedule an appointment with your child's pediatrician about your concerns.
4. Understand that if your doctor recommends your child see a psychiatrist, it is because these doctors specialize in mental health treatments.
5. If medications are recommended, remember that these medication simply help to stimulate the neurobiological chemicals that are genetically absent for your child.
6. Know that medication is not magic. Your child may still need help with academic or social strategies.

~Laurie Dupar, PMHNP, RN, PCC

Laurie Dupar, Nurse Practitioner, Senior Certified ADHD Coach, Laurie@CoachingforADHD.com www.CoachingforADHD.com

"Aim for success, not perfection. Never give up your right to be wrong, because then you will lose the ability to learn new things and move forward with your life."

~Dr. David M. Burns

Stimulating vs. Non-Stimulating

Think of tasks as either stimulating or non-stimulating. Stimulating tasks are the ones I want to do. Non-stimulating tasks are the ones I start of "kind of" not wanting to do, then I really don't want to do, and then I avoid until the pain of not doing them becomes stimulating enough to force me into action. This can include something as "simple" as opening the mail. Forcing ourselves through a non-stimulating task is fraught with stress and pain. Instead, add stimulation. Make it a game, break it into pieces, or include things you enjoy. It will make progress more sustainable and less painful!

~Ian King, Speaker

Ian King, Coach/Speaker specializing in ADHD and gifted adults, children, families, and entrepreneurs. Past President of ADHD Coaches Organization & ICF Chicago www.KingSolutionsInc.com

Lying and ADHD

Lying is stress management in the moment when confronted.

People lie to protect themselves from getting into trouble or feeling shame. They are quick on their feet with lies but slow with the truth.

Lying can be attention-getting and inflating. It becomes habituated, developing a disconnect between what is real versus imagination/fantasy.

Kids need to be taught that honesty trumps getting into trouble. In coming clean, it gets them out of the vicious cycle that keeps them stuck. Parents can use the cue of "clean slate" to spark the brain to pause and think with the mind's eye.

~Fran Parker, PhD

A fully licensed Psychologist and Coordinator of EOC CHADD in MI. The Award Recipient for 2010 from CHADD in teaching the Parent-to-Parent Classes.

Good Enough

Perfectionism is a common ADHD trait. I am thrilled I learned the concept of "good enough." I know I am not perfect, and whatever I create or do is never going to be perfect, no matter how much time I spend trying to make it that way. I used to spend hours editing everything I wrote, redoing things I made, stopping and replaying measures of piano music over and over, rather than continuing to play when I made a mistake. Now, I no longer do that. I know I am good enough and whatever I do is, too!

~Dee Doochin, MLAS

Dee Doochin, MLAS, Professional Certified Coach, Certified Mentor Coach, Senior Certified ADHD Coach, wife, mother, grandmother, great-grandmother with ADHD, adventurer, lover of life! www.addupcoach.com

Siblings and ADHD

The impact on siblings of children with ADHD is not often talked about. Studies show that siblings of children with ADHD experience the same disruption, chaos, unpredictability and exhaustion as their parents. At times they may feel victimized, unprotected and powerless, particularly when faced with expectations to "take care" of their sibling. A healthy family considers everyone's needs.

Here are some tips for parents to minimize the effects on their children without ADHD:

- Watch for victimization...it is not the same as rivalry.
- Minimize expectations of another child taking care of their ADHD sibling; you are the parent, not them.
- Listen and act when one of your other children report aggression from their ADHD sibling.
- Make the time and effort to spend time and appreciate your other children.

~Laurie Dupar, PMHNP, RN, PCC

Laurie Dupar, Senior Certified ADHD Coach www.CoachingforADHD.com

But Mom, I Cant' Do My Homework Without My Music!

Listening to familiar music can actually help sustain attention. It both supports alertness and helps create a "fence" around your attention so you're not as distracted by other sounds. If your music bothers those around you, use headphones. If music isn't your thing, try a desktop program or smartphone app like Ambiance or WhiteNoise.

~Roland Rotz, Ph.D.

Dr. Roland Rotz, Ph.D., and Coach Sarah D. Wright, M.S., A.C.T., internationally-known authors, speakers, and ADHD experts. www.FidgetToFocus.com

Yes I Can

At times it's easy to get trapped in a negative cycle. Affirmations can be a great help when trying to let go of negative thoughts and change the direction of our day. Many of us wake up and look in the mirror and begin pulling ourselves, our bodies and our lives apart. Instead, write down some positive affirmations about yourself, such as; "I am a good person," "I am a loving mother," or "I am a dedicated worker." Post these on mirrors, doors, refrigerators and other places around the house where you will see them. Better yet, speak them out loud. You won't help but start to notice positive changes in your thoughts and experiences throughout the day.

~Anonymous

55 Positive ADHD Characteristics

People with ADHD are amazing. In the right environment, with encouragement and support, their strengths grow, and the possibilities to show their positive qualities increases. This list of is a compilation from three workshops for ADHD adults...it has changed peoples lives.

1. Swift 2. Resilient 3. Flexible 4. Persistent 5. Non-hesitant 6. Result-oriented 7. Innovative 8. Managerially-skilled 9. Caring 10. Amiable 11. Charming 12. Humorous 13. Objective at emergencies 14. Fearless 15. Promotes change 16. Non-linear 17. Out-of-the-box thinker 18. Rapidly associative 19. Sprinter 20. Intuitive 21. Sociable 22. Creative 23. Engaged 24. Loyal 25. Outspoken 26.Energetic 27. Independent 28. Individualistic 29. Spontaneous 30. Able to hyperfocus 31. Loving 32. Sharp 33. Persistent 34. Eager 35. Has incentive 36. Ambitious 37. Visionary 38. Strong personality 39. Quick-witted 40. Fast-forward thinkers 41. Lateral thinkers 42. Living in the now 43. Hopeful 44. Helpful 45. Vigorous 46. Emotional 47. Passionate 48.Scans the surroundings 49. Fast getting the overview 50. Impulsive 51. Strategic 52. Curious 53. Resourceful 54.Imaginative 55. Courageous

~Marie Enback, ADHD Coach

Marie Enback, first ADHD Coach in Sweden and initiator of ADHD Awareness Week Sweden. Conference organizer, writer, speaker and educator. www.adhdcoaching.se www.lateralia.se www.adhdawarenessweek.se

Train Your Brain

Think before you click. That's the motto I use for my favorite brain-training software. Utilizing an online program, you can improve your impulsivity, attention and focus with simple cognitive exercises. Rather than overwhelming you with multiple stimuli like many video games do, brain-training software improves your process of responding quickly but accurately. It forces you to zero in on one task and filter out other distractions. Most of my clients find their attention and focus improve significantly after working with this kind of software. It's fun, easy, affordable and takes very little time.

~Dr. Billi, Ph.D.

The AttentionB Method, Neuro-Cognitive Behavioral Therapy/Coaching with Dr. Billi, Ph.D. Take a Step Toward Your Peak Potential. Schedule a Coaching Session Now. www.AttentionB.com DrBilli@AttentionB.com (855) DrBilli

Raising Ethical Children

Establish Ground Rules in your home and in your family relationships. Be clear about the kind of family you are and how you expect your children to treat those within and outside of your family.

Model Compassion. Emphasize caring, compassion and giving.

Teach Respect. Keep in mind that teaching your children respect for others is one of the best gifts you can give them.

Talk, Collaborate and Make Decisions Together. Model and teach about better choices when your kids are calm.

Be Firm Yet Loving. Clear boundaries and consistent responses inspire better behavior and create safety and security for kids and teens.

Give Your Time, Not Toys. There is nothing your child wants more than you.

~Lynne Kenney, PsyD

Lynne Kenney, PsyD, provides helping skills and strategies on The Parenting Team. Learn more at www.lynnekenney.com

ADHD, Most People Just Don't Get It!!!

I can't tell you how important it is to continually educate yourself about your ADHD. Because ADHD shows up so differently in everyone, it is often misunderstood, including by the ADHDers themselves.

Understanding your ADHD and communicating it to family and friends is important so they "get" why you struggle with so-called "easy" tasks or why you often can't help doing the things you do.

When others understand, they will cut you some slack and help keep you on track and accountable, without you feeling like a failure.

So, learn about your ADHD, understand your ADHD, then celebrate your ADHD!

~Joey Bishop, ADHD Life Coach

Joey Bishop, ADD/ADHD Life Coach www.ADDvanceforward.com

Advice for Parents

Rules I follow:

1. Believe! When a child says, "I didn't mean to," "I forgot," "I did listen," or "I work better with the music," believe them; it's true!
2. Listen. When they yell, "it's too loud," "I get it," or "Okay!" They are overloaded. Stop.
3. Show them HOW; they need to see it!
4. Explain it their way; your way won't work.
5. Practice! They can't do it hearing or seeing it just once.
6. Know that paying attention, when it doesn't come naturally, is a struggle.

~Sandy Alletto Corbin, M.A., SCAC

Ms. Sandy Alletto Corbin, M.A., SCAC, Certified Senior ADHD Coach and Advocate working with families, teens and women. She can be reached at http://www.lifecoachsandyalletto.com

Flex Your Muscles!

Self-control is a muscle. It is strengthened by using it. Consider exercising your self-control, i.e. willpower to build your capacity.

Like working out with free weights, choose a task for which you have some resistance, but not too much. Strength is gained through repetition. Start by sitting up straight each time you think about it. Next time you think about it add the next step. Then the next. This task will get easier with repetition, in only a week or two. Other tasks requiring willpower will be easier also.

Some people with ADHD like to change their "work out" and start with the challenging tasks first…then everything else is easy!

~Kathy Peterson, ADHD Coach

Kathy Peterson, ADHD Coach since 1994, works with adults, professionals, entrepreneurs, and people in corporate business and science; Arlington, MA; credentialed by ICF www.petersoncoaching.com

Success for the College Student

Lost phone, piles on desk, can't find those notes from class? For college students with ADHD, keeping things organized will help you stay focused and efficient.

- Use a "launching and landing" pad – a place to put everything that you carry in and out of your room (keys, cell phone, books, planner, etc.).
- Have all supplies in a drawer or basket near your study space.
- Have lots of clocks in view and timers ready.
- Use a three-ring binder for each class, containing syllabus, notes & handouts in order by date and lined paper. Re-organize weekly.

~Casey Dixon, MSEd, CTACC

Casey Dixon, MSEd, CTACC www.dixonlifecoaching.com

Test and Performance Anxiety

Test and performance anxieties are real!

Dr. Daniel Amen's brain SPECT scans (one at rest and one while stressed) vividly demonstrate that when you are anxious, overwhelmed or panicked, the color-coded computer printout shows the Anterior Cingulate Gyrus and Basal Ganglia (anxiety) are red (hot) and the Pre-Frontal Cortex (memory) is white (not working.) Blue is normal.

Picture a garage door slamming shut with all the useful information inside. A way to keep the garage door open and information accessible when you're stressed is to take 5-10 slow, deep breaths.

Voila! You can think again!

~Victoria Ball, M.ED, MCC, SCAC

Victoria Ball, ADD Career Coach, specializes in identifying successful college/career choices and life/work/productivity management strategies www.ADDventuresinliving.com
(401) 272-0435

How to Get to Bed at a Reasonable Time

Here are some tips:

- Go to bed when another grown-up does. Even if you think you get a lot done when they're not there, what is the quality of that work?
- Don't read a page-turner book. Do read a long magazine article.
- If you play computer solitaire before bed, I bet you can see the cards laid out on the inside of your eyes in the dark. Not helpful.
- Don't drink too much water right before bed. ...DUH!
- Don't eat before bed. A full stomach requires digestion. That takes energy and isn't really relaxing!

~Kerch McConlogue ,PCC, CPCC

Kerch McConlogue, PCC, CPCC, works with adults in Baltimore and around the world who have ADHD. Find her on the web at www.mapthefuture.com

Seeing the "Big Picture"

Are you haunted by procrastination? Here's an idea: start with a picture!

Why a picture? The source of procrastination is often not having a clear picture of what you need to do. You may be confused. You may think the task is either too hard and too scary to start, or so simple that you don't need to start yet.

The solution is to start drawing because many people with ADHD are visual learners. Your drawing can be very simple, with stick figures and symbolic images. When you see the "big picture" with all of its pieces, you know where to start.

~Laurie Senders, Ph.D.

Laurie Senders, Ph.D. www.compellingADHDcoach.com

Ways to Improve Communication

It can be quite challenging being an ADHD-parent of an ADHD-teenager. We have learned to communicate in different ways when talking about difficult issues, such as:

- Taking the car for a ride through the forest while counting the deer
- Going for an ice cream or a snack
- Going to a well-known place to help your ADHD-teenager relax

Even though my son is no longer a teenager, he still asks to go for a ride when he feels like talking. After an argument, we message each other on Skype or use our cell phones to break the ice and solve the problems.

~Charlotte Hjorth, ADHD Coach

Charlotte Hjorth is the first Professional ADHD Coach in Denmark, initiator of the ADHD Awareness Week Denmark in 2008, supervisor, writer, speaker, and educator www.adhd-coaching.dk

Fidgeting – Your Secret Weapon!

Any activity that is both mindless and is something you do when you are also doing something else is what we call a "fidget." Common fidgets include pacing, twirling a pen, doodling on paper, listening to music, or chewing gum while also thinking, listening, reading, writing, or doing homework.

Fidgeting can help you pay attention by adding sensory stimulation to any activity, which can in turn help your brain be more focused and alert. Many of these fidgets can be done very discreetly, so you can manage your ADHDness without anyone even noticing.

Fidgeting can be your secret weapon!

~Sarah D. Wright, M.S., A.C.T.

Roland Rotz, Ph.D. and Coach Sarah D. Wright, M.S., A.C.T., internationally-known authors, speakers, and ADHD experts. www.FidgetToFocus.com

What's Your "Study Style"?

Many people know their "learning style": they are a visual, auditory, kinesthetic or tactile learner. However, knowing your "study style" or where/how/when you do your best work or learning is equally valuable. To figure out your "study style," ask yourself:

- Do I focus best in a quiet environment or where there is some background noise/activity?
- Do I like everything spread around me or pay attention better in a tidy environment?
- Do I learn best alone or with others?
- When do I do my "best"? In the morning/afternoon/early evening/night?

The answers to these questions can help you understand how you learn best and know your "study style".

~Laurie Dupar, PMHNP, RN, PCC

Laurie Dupar, Senior Certified ADHD Coach, www.CoachingforADHD.com

The Gift of Being ADHD

You have a gift if you have ADHD. Why? Because you have the unique ability to take in more information and stimulation than most people. These qualities give you the ability to hyperfocus on a particular project and work with greater speed than many of your peers. You can see the way to manage, build, or create while so many others are still contemplating the possibilities. Not you! You are often already in action, getting it done with unmatched speed, endurance and determination.

Leverage this gift! So many others have! (Google Search: ADHD Famous People.)

~Judith A. Cahall, M.S.

Judith A. Cahall, M.S., Partnerships for Personal Change. ADHD and Life Coaching emphasizing the principles of Positive Psychology and Appreciative Living. Nationally Certified School Psychologist. StarfishAllianceCoaching@gmail.com

Mine Your Experiences

Get in the habit of ALWAYS reviewing the results of a project, paper, or test.

When you "mine" your experiences, you find new ways to be successful the next time you have a similar assignment. What went well? What didn't go well? What was a disappointment? What will you change in the future?

After you do your "mining," write your learning down in a place that you will be able to access it as you prepare for your next exciting project. Then, before you start, spend a few minutes to review all that "gold."

~Dema K. Stout, M.A., PCC, CPCC

Dema Stout M.A., PCC, CPCC, Master's educated, Professional Certified Coach and graduate of Coaches Training Institute with specialized training in ADHD www.synergycoach.com

Behavior and Productivity: Sometimes it's a Tradeoff

Ever notice that sometimes pushing your child to work harder increases tension but not productivity? Regardless of what you think they SHOULD handle, they may not be Response-ABLE yet.

Slower processing speed and deficits in executive functioning sometimes make actions difficult for them. Your judging, anger, even positive rewards may do little to motivate and may actually trigger rebellious behavior.

Try this: let go and be willing to partner with your child on a slower, more manageable path. Be there to model or sometimes just accompany as a grounding presence. Your trusting, close relationship will promote greater, healthier growth over time.

~Cindy Goldrich, Ed. M., ACAC

Cindy Goldrich, Ed. M., ACAC, Certified ADHD Parent Coach
www.PTScoaching.com Cindy@PTScoaching.com
(516) 802-0593 Coaching available in New York and Telephone.
Parent the Child YOU have!

Stepping Stones Out of Stumbling Blocks

"I haven't succeeded in school in spite of my difficulties, but probably because of them."

ADHD coaching made all the difference for this successful college student. Coaching helped him recognize what was most difficult for him (and why), as well as how to use his strengths to design effective workarounds. With the help of his coach, he developed goals and designed action plans to realize them.

It's common to see ADHD as an obstacle, but it doesn't have to be. As Jack Penn pointed out,"One of the secrets of life is to make stepping stones out of stumbling blocks."

~Roxanne Fouche, ADHD Coach

Roxanne Fouche, ADHD Coach and Consultant, specializes in working with individuals of all ages with ADHD/LD and related challenges.
(858) 484-4749 www.FocusForEffectiveness.com/blog
Roxanne@RoxanneFouche.com

"You will come to know the way to success only when you know your strengths and also the way in which they can help you and others for a good purpose."

~Varun Saurya A

Label Everything!

Best $50 you'll ever spend: buy a Brother P-touch labeler. Then get ready to plaster your life with labels: cabinet drawers, phone headset, copier (with instructions), cell phone, notebooks, tires (with PSI requirements), electrical circuit box, garden tools, storage containers, transformers for computer equipment, shoe boxes, mobile phones (to show which room they live in), silverware tray, spice rack, birdfeeder (with recipe for hummingbird nectar). And oh, yeah: file folders. The list is endless. But don't label your kids or your spouse or partner. They don't like it.

~Linda Roggli, PCC,CLC

Linda Roggli, PCC/CLC Professional Certified Coach, Author of *"Confessions of an ADDiva: midlife in the non-linear lane"*
http://confessionsofanaddiva.net

Pay Attention to Me!

In a conversation, involve yourself in what the other person is saying. Put aside what you are doing for the moment; if you aren't able to put aside what you are doing, reassure the other person that what they have to say is indeed important to you. This shows them that you want to give them your full attention so you can focus on their words. Let them know that you may need a couple of minutes to shift from what you were doing so you can sit down to talk with them.

~Laurie Moore Skillings, SCAC

Laurie Moore Skillings, Senior Certified ADHD Coach, specializes in working with teens that have a hard time with school.. Laurie can be reached at laurie@addwithease.com

S.T.A.R.T. Me Up

Can't seem to get started on a project or task? Follow S.T.A.R.T. and overcome procrastination!

- **S**peak a commitment to your task out loud
- **T**hree initial steps
- **A**cknowledge fear or resistance
- **R**espond with love and lasting benefits
- **T**ime to Tackle

S "I commit to cleaning my bedroom."
T Write and say the first 3 steps needed.
A "I notice I fear it will never be done right."
R Send love and compassion to the fear and resistance. Name a lasting benefit(s) when accomplished: "I'll sleep better in a clutter-free room."
T Set TIME, take initial three steps and TACKLE the TASK!

Repeat (any) steps as necessary.

~Melissa R. Fahrney, M.A., CPC

Melissa Fahrney, M.A., CPC, ADHD/Stress Management Coach for kids, college students & adults "Don't stress out, master your mountain, with heart!" www.ADDHeartWorks.com www.facebook.com/addheartworks (888) 327-5727

How to Survive the Freshman Year

- Avoid overwhelm by breaking your projects down into sizeable chunks.
- Get yourself a study buddy.
- Be accountable to someone, such as a friend or a classmate.
- Reach out to friends and/or professors when you need help.
- Use one portable calendar both for school and personal appointments.
- Get enough sleep.
- Take afternoon classes if you are not a morning person.
- Plan ahead for your tests and projects.
- Check your calendar daily.
- Don't slack off in the beginning. If you start off strong, you will be better off in the end.

~Roya Kravetz

Roya Kravetz, Life Coach/parent instructor, specializes in coaching and consulting with youth and adults with ADHD regarding ADHD and/or related challenges

Shared Success

- Is learning in a group something you enjoy?
- Are you someone who benefits from listening to others share their experiences?
- Do you want to connect with other adults who are going through similar challenges with ADHD?

Join an ADHD Support Group! Group are often facilitated by ADHD Coaches and meet via a telephone bridge line, so you can participate no matter where you are in the world. Most ADHD/ADD support groups alternate between discussion on current ADHD issues and brief coaching opportunities for participants. The perfect member is someone over 18 years old and diagnosed with ADHD/ADD or who cares about someone with ADHD/ADD...that simple!

~Laurie Dupar, PMHNP, RN, PCC

ADDults in Action Group facilitated by Laurie Dupar, ADHD Coach, meets on the first and third Wednesday of the month. www.CoachingforADHD.com

Welcome to a New Year!

Are you kidding? What's welcoming about the return of last year's "gremlins"? You know, those pesky negative voices we hear in our heads. They remind us that "we shoud have studied more...should have taken better notes...we won't remember a thing or it's too late now."

Instead, close your eyes, thank them for their input and send them on their way. You are at a different place this year! Erase and clean your mental whiteboard. What do you want to write on it? Set intentions and write down the steps that will help you achieve them! Hear the new positive empowering voices? "I am able, all is well."

~Ana Sánchez, Life Coach

Ana Sánchez, sassy,authentic & witty mom, wife, Certified ADHD Life Coach, friend, lawyer, passionate explorer of strengths. Curious about possibilities from 'I'm Able' stance.

What Do You Choose? Help or Quit?

Sharing a lesson on choice..... After making the decision to return to college for my bachelor's degree when I was in my late 30's, I started off "slow and steady" with only one course per semester and then gradually increased to full-time college studies. When challenges occurred, and they did, I had a CHOICE to make; I could continue on my journey and ask for help or quit as I had in the past. Although quitting was my default and it was very familiar for me to hide behind my truth of fear, shame and things being too hard, I chose to no longer live that way. "I asked for help"...

~Cindy Giardina, PCC

Cindy Giardina, PCC, ADHD Coach, Diagnosed with ADHD/LD at age 42 while in college, graduating with honors 3 years later. Contact Coach Cindy: cindy@kaleidoscope-coaching.com (973) 694-5077

Create Your Good Mood

Have you noticed that when you feel happy, you might smile or sing or be kind and then you feel even better about yourself, and that the cycle repeats? Similarly, when you are crabby, you're likely to stomp around, slam doors and snap at people and then you feel worse about yourself, and that cycle repeats too? Congratulations, you've recognized that humans have circular wiring. But, did you know you are not a victim to those cycles, and you can interrupt them at any time? In a bad mood, make yourself smile, say something nice, or sing, and your mood will change.

~Cindy Lea, M.A.

Cindy Lea, M.A., Psychotherapist, and ADD Coach & Speaker. Inspiring others by focusing on strengths and possibilities with warmth & humor. Minneapolis, MN (612) 965-3052
www.SucceedingWithADD.com Cindy@succeedingwithadd.com

No Smoking

Many ADHD people self-medicate through alcohol, drugs and smoking. Yes, I put smoking in the same group as drugs because nicotine is an addictive substance. While it may calm you temporarily, it will kill you in the end. 50% of ADHD people smoke, and it hurts them in more than the obvious medical ways. And once you start, it is hard to quit. Among the non-medical ways smoking hurts are that it often defines who becomes and stays your friends, whether you get a job or get picked for an athletic team. It is simple: don't start, even if some of your peers do.

~Abigail Wurf, M.Ed.

ADHD Coach Abigail Wurf, M.Ed. My life experience/training make me confident that together, we can make a positive difference in your life! www.abigailwurf.com, awurf@verizon.net (202) 244-2234

Facing Reality

Sometimes the focus that ADHD medication creates isn't entirely pleasant. A client just beginning treatment once told me, "Y'know, before the drug, I could ignore my wife's hurtful comments fairly easily. Now, they don't fly by … they stick." If you use meds as part of your ADHD treatment plan, don't stop them to avoid facing painful realities. Instead, work with a therapist to learn how to cope with your emotional challenges, integrate your medicated and unmedicated selves, and mold your life into what you want it to be.

~Debbie Stanley, LLPC, NCC, CPO-CD

Debbie Stanley is a licensed mental health counselor specializing in chronic disorganization and hoarding, both of which often co-occur with ADHD. www.thoughtsinorder.com

College + ADHD = Success

You can be successful in college with ADHD by following these tips:

- Seek help from your college's Disabilities Office
- Work to your strengths.
- Use personalized strategies matching your learning style.
- Ensure balance in your life; don't just focus on studying.
- Consider an accountability buddy.
- Set realistic goals, using small steps at a time.
- Break down assignments into manageable chunks, with a deadline for each piece.
- Use technology that works for you.
- Reduce distractions in class; silence your phone, not just on vibrate.

~Rose Steele, RN, PhD

Rose Steele, RN, PhD, www.AdultADDCoaching.ca

F.E.T.I.D.S.

Do you find yourself attempting to do too much, with too little time?

Adults with ADHD frequently have a horrible time with effective planning and scheduling.

I have coined this phenomena F.E.T.I.D.S.

"**F**uture **E**vent **T**ime **I**nterval **D**istortion **S**yndrome" (definition): the inability to plan independent future events without a distorted perspective of time interval between events.

You can manage F.E.T.I.D.S. by practicing simple planning strategies:

- Use a calendar.
- Schedule transition time between events.
- Avoid over-scheduling and always schedule extra time into your day to borrow from later in case some tasks require more time than originally planned.

~Coach Rudy Rodriguez, LCSW

Coach Rudy Rodriguez, began working with ADHD in 1981 and was diagnosed with ADHD in 1983. He is the Founder of 'ADHD Center for Success

Be Your Own Advocate

As a person with ADHD, you are unique. Be proud of who you are. Don't compare yourself to others. Celebrate your individuality. People may paint you to be "odd." Teach them to respect you for what you are, not what you aren't. There is a quote by Emerson that encourages people to create their own path, for those who walk on the same path get to the same place. This isn't a license to disobey laws or break rules. Be aware that the way you do things is usually not the way others do them. But when you are willing to embrace your uniqueness, do it fully.

~Dr. Billi, Ph.D.

The AttentionB Method, Expressive Arts Therapy/Coaching with Dr. Billi, Ph.D. Outsmart your ADHD with my Creative Tools and Strategies. Preserve your Uniqueness. (855) DrBilli
www.AttentionB.com DrBilli@AttentionB.com

"Dopamine Boosters"

There is a great deal of misinformation about ADHD "stimulant" medications. One I frequently hear is the confusion about why you would give a 'stimulant' to someone who is "hyperactive." The answer is often surprising. With ADHD medications, what is being "stimulated" is the neurotransmitter dopamine, hence the term "Dopamine Booster." Dopamine is the main neurotransmitter that is either available in insufficient amounts or being used ineffectively in people diagnosed with ADHD. When someone takes a stimulant medication, it helps to increase the amount/and or usefulness of the dopamine now available for the part of our brain that helps us stop, sit still, pause, and keep our attention on things less interesting.

~Laurie Dupar, PMHNP, RN, PCC

Laurie Dupar, PMHNP, Certified ADHD Coach, specializes in helping you understand your brain, navigate the treatment maze, reduce your challenges and get things done! www.CoachingforADHD.com

Five Easy Pieces

Paper is my major challenge...it is everywhere! I can't read on a computer, so I print things out and have a hard time throwing them away. I file vertically – on my desk, on my table, on the floor, on the cabinets, etc. I am not totally of the "out of sight, out of mind school," but almost. Keeping up with the clutter is a HUGE job. Therefore, ***each*** time I enter my office, I pick up and deal with at least five pieces of paper, putting them into the file bin or into the recycling/trash.

~Dee Doochin, MLAS

Dee Doochin, MLAS, Professional Certified Coach, Certified Mentor Coach, Senior Certified ADHD Coach, wife, mother, grandmother, great-grandmother with ADHD, adventurer, lover of life! www.addupcoach.com

Words of Inspiration

Forgive Yourself ~ Feel Hopeful ~ Find Solutions ~ Move Forward.

Know that ADHD is about difference - not less!

Remember, it's not how you get there, but that you find the success you desire.

It is important to foster the feeling of "I can do it" in children, adolescents, adults and yourself --- to find inspiration for that unique personal greatness.

It is about putting on those new wings and learning how to fly!

~Beverly Rohman, SCAC

Beverly Rohman, founder of The Learning Connections LLC, Senior Certified ADHD Coach and Learning Consultant working with families, adults, college students, professionals. Easton, MD www.thelearningconnections.net

Getting Homework to College

Whenever possible, arrange with teachers ahead of time to be able to send any homework or correspondence between student and school via e-mail as an attachment. Many teachers have computers and cell phones. Forgetting homework is a big source of frustration for students and a classic ADHD symptom. Usually when one assignment is forgotten, things pile up, grades fall and students drop the course. It's simple; if you have to be reminded, enlist a friend. Scan or photograph the work with your cell and send it right to the teacher's e-mail.

~Sandy Alletto Corbin, M.A., SCAC

Ms. Sandy Alletto Corbin, M.A., SCAC, Certified Senior ADHD Coach and Advocate working with families, teens and women. She can be reached at www.lifecoachsandyalletto.com

Find the Trickle

When faced with a task, people with ADHD can become daunted at the mere thought of starting. Find your path to action by visualizing a crack in a dam that allows a small trickle of water (your creative ability). When the trickle is allowed to flow without judgment, after a short period of time it will gain momentum, becoming a serious leak until the dam that is holding you back from completing your task crumbles and the water (your creativity) rages forward. So, when stuck, find your trickle, withhold judgment, let the trickle flow, and you might be amazed by what follows!

~Ian King, Coach/Speaker

Ian King, Coach/Speaker specializing in ADHD and gifted adults, children, families, and entrepreneurs. Past President of ADHD Coaches Organization & ICF Chicago. www.KingSolutionsInc.com

When Less is More!

Repeating everything to your children over and over again is like a vaccine that immunizes your children's ears against your words!

In order to really get your children to listen, try talking less and giving your child doable choices. Make what you say count and be consistent with the consequences. Say, for example, "Johnny, time to get ready for bed," while pointing to the clock. Then help them feel in control by giving them a choice, such as, "Johnny, do you want to brush your teeth or put on your pj's first?" Having a win-win simple choice engages your child and gets the desired task accomplished.

~Roya Kravetz, ADHD Coach

Roya Kravetz, Credentialed Life Coach, ADHD Coach and Consultant, and Parent Educator. Specializes in ADHD Coaching and/or related challenges. www.adhdsuccesscoaching.com

Take Breaks on Time

I used to get annoyed when my teens would say, "I am taking a break." But they may have been on to something. Taking a break actually increases your productivity. If I have to tackle an unpleasant or tedious task, I set a timer for 30 minutes. Knowing a break is on the horizon, and I won't be doing this task for hours, gives me the motivation to focus on it. Using a timer on days when I am really distracted also pulls me back on task if my mind has wandered.

~Karen Peak, CPA

Karen Peak - not your typical certified public accountant - runs a successful tax and bookkeeping practice in Northern California, helping entrepreneurial clients from coast to coast. www.karenpeakcpa.com

There is No Such Thing as an ADHD-Friendly College

A college may have the best student services in the world, but if a student isn't organized enough to take advantage of them, they might as well not be there. College life puts such huge demands on executive functioning that all college students exhibit more ADHD-like behaviors than non-college students. The best thing you can do to get off to a good start or get back on track is to get a coach who specializes in working with college students with ADHD. A coach can cost a lot less than a failed course or "lost" semester!

~Sarah D. Wright, M.S., A.C.T.

Sarah D. Wright, M.S., A.C.T., internationally-known ADHD coach, speaker, author, expert, and founding Board Member of the ADHD Coaches Organization. Contact her at Sarah@FocusForEffectiveness.com

"If A equals success, then the formula is A equals X plus Y and Z, with X being work, Y play, and Z keeping your mouth shut."

~Albert Einstein

Nutritional Testing for ADHD

Medical evidence supports the role of certain nutrients for brain function, though nutritional advice for ADHD is overwhelming. There is no "one size fits all" nutrient guideline, and taking handfuls of supplements can be dangerous if you don't need them. Specific testing is available to evaluate your functional deficiencies for nutrients that are critical to brain function, including essential fatty acids, essential amino acids, vitamins, minerals, antioxidants, and omega 3 fatty acids. Every process in the body requires specific nutrients, so make sure poor nutrition is not affecting your mood or attention issues.

~Dr. Susan Wilder

Dr. Susan Wilder, CEO of LifeScape Medical Associates and LifeScape Premier, expert in nutritional testing and interventions for mood/attention problems in adults and children. www.lifescapepremier.com (480) 860-5269

The Other Side of Your Front Door

I had a friend who couldn't figure out why things weren't improving in her life as she wanted, until she realized that she was spending most of her time trying to fix it from the inside of her front door! Isolation can take us to dark places and get us caught in a negative spiral of thoughts. Try not to isolate yourself too much in your day. Of course, time to yourself is important, but if this goes on day after day you are not giving yourself a chance to encounter any positive and interesting new experiences. Walk out the front door, do something, interact with others. Your life is waiting.

~Anonymous

Trick it Out

Create a door hanger or poster(s) with each step of your children's daily routine in a picture or words, with morning on the front and nighttime on the back. Then, teach them to navigate on their own with a reward system in place for getting everything done!

~Robin Nordmeyer, ADHD Coach

ADHD Coach, Robin Nordmeyer www.LifeAheadCoaching.com

Fishing for Ideas

Think of the steady stream of ideas you have like a flowing river filled with beautiful fish. You can dip your hand into the water at any time and grab a fish or many fish. All the fish (ideas) are beautiful, but which one will provide the tastiest meal for you right now? Keep that one and enjoy it fully! Use that great idea to create something wonderful. Let the other fish go on downstream for another fisherman or another day. When you're hungry again, you can go to the endless stream of sparkling fish for your next tasty meal. Yum!

~Barbara Luther, MCC

Barbara Luther, Master ADHD Certified Coach, www.WindBeneathYourWings.com President, Professional Association of ADHD Coaches, www.PAACCoaches.org Director of Training, ADD Coach Academy, www.addca.com www.SoaringCoachesCircle.com St. Louis, MO, (573) 340-3559

Managing Projects with ADHD

Do projects overwhelm you? Are they difficult to start? Projects, big and small, can be overwhelming for a student or adult with ADHD. Try these steps to get started:

First, list all the steps you need to complete. Do this over a couple of days to make sure you capture everything.

Second, decide in which order the tasks need to be completed. You might adjust the order later, but it will help to prioritize from the beginning.

Third, put a date next to each task and commit to a start date.

What project can you use to test drive this concept?

~Laura Rolands, ADHD Coach

Laura Rolands is an Attention and ADHD Coach who helps students and adults pay attention and increase productivity. Connect with Laura at www.MyAttentionCoach.com or www.Twitter.com/CoachforADHD

Don't Wait for the Yearly Review

As an ADHD employee, you may need exact, frequent and immediate feedback. Talk with your supervisor to see if you can have weekly meetings. Let your supervisor know that you would like to start the meetings with positive comments and then work through any negative comments to find solutions. This will keep you on track for success.

~Robb Garrett, MA, MCC, ACT

Robb Garrett, MA, MCC, ACT, President of ADHD Coaches Organization www.adhdcoaches.org

You are Your Child's First Coach

ADHD coaches can help their clients understand their ADHD so they can successfully create and use strategies to reach their goals, whether they are academic, social, professional or personal. As a parent, you are your child's first coach. Help your children understand how their brain works best. What works and what doesn't. What are their strengths, where are their challenges. Read, ask, and learn about different strategies to help your children better manage their challenges and enjoy their strengths so they can feel successful, happy and confident about themselves.

~Laurie Dupar, Certified ADHD Coach

Laurie Dupar, PMHNP, Certified ADHD Coach, specializes in helping you understand your brain, navigate the treatment maze, reduce your challenges and get things done! www.CoachingforADHD.com

The Power of Now

Sometimes the stress and strain of ADHD can make life difficult.

This disorder can be accompanied by chaos, confusion, and serious consequences. It is easy to get overwhelmed and stuck in negativity. We may feel like the problem is unsolvable and the damage is permanent.

One trick to calm down and start problem-solving is to tack the word "now" onto negative thoughts. i.e. "we are having financial trouble (now)" or "my daughter is acting out (now)" or "my boss is unreasonable (now)."

It is easier to resolve issues from a perspective that they will not last and that change is possible.

~ Marie Paxson, CHADD Immediate Past President

Marie Paxson, parent, advocate, and past CHADD President

Succeeding in College

College can be particularly challenging for students with ADHD because academic expectations increase while there is a simultaneous decrease in external structure. Students may have difficulty prioritizing competing demands on their time, as there are varying class times and new daily routines. Even if it wasn't necessary in high school, many college students find it extremely useful to use paper or digital planners to map out their days, scheduling the actual times that they plan to accomplish their goals: going to class or work, studying, eating, sleeping, doing laundry and other errands, exercising and/or enjoying social activities.

~Roxanne Fouche, ADHD Coach

Roxanne Fouche, ADHD Coach/Consultant, specializes in working with individuals of all ages with ADHD/LD and related challenges
www.FocusForEffectiveness.com/blog
(858) 484-4749 Roxanne@FocusForEffectiveness.com

Why Don't They Like Me?

It's sad to see children rejected because of poor social skills! Children and adults with ADHD often monopolize conversations, talk excessively and barely listen to others. Social skills counseling can help improve relationships with friends, family and colleagues! Some tips include:

1. Listen while others speak.
2. Take turns in conversations.
3. Learn to read non-verbal cues when interacting with others.
4. Stand an appropriate distance from others.
5. Don't interrupt private conversations.
6. Don't yell out answers in class.
7. Have good eye contact.
8. Think about what to say before you say it.
9. Don't disrupt the class or meetings at work.

~Lisa-Anne Ray-Byers

Lisa-Anne Ray-Byers, Speech-Language Pathologist, Columnist and Author, www.AskLisaAnne.com

Medication Reminder

Even once-a-day meds don't work unless they're taken, and we all have those scattered mornings! But you almost always have your purse or your wallet. Purses can hold last month's medication bottle(s) with a few pills. And guys, it's surprising how well a couple of pills will stay intact in the corners of your wallet. Remember, you need a label with that bottle! Don't be without that label of legitimacy. So, whatever the medication, tape that duplicate pharmacy label they gave you onto an index card and keep it in there with the pills.

~John I. Bailey, Jr., MD

John I. Bailey, Jr., MD, Center for Attention & Learning,
Mobile, AL, adddoc@bellsouth.net

Avoiding Crisis with Time Management

Many people with ADHD struggle with managing time. Often they're running late, double booking themselves or forgetting appointments altogether. "Crisis mode" usually ensues – that frantic feeling of rushing from here to there and back again. The easiest solution: use an online calendar. Sync it with all electronic devices. Color code appointments. Use automatic text message and email reminders. Allow a 30-minute space in between appointments. Schedule appointment times as well as times you need to leave for appointments. Don't forget to schedule in things you enjoy. Also, put a clock in the bathroom and set all clocks 15 minutes fast.

~Dr. Billi, Ph.D.

The AttentionB Method, Neuro-Cognitive Behavioral Therapy/Coaching with Dr. Billi, Ph.D. Working with Your ADHD to Preserve your Uniqueness. www.AttentionB.com DrBilli@AttentionB.com (855) DrBilli

Follow the Bouncing Ball

Working with children with ADHD at home or in school can be a challenge due to their restlessness.

Here's an idea:

Purchase a large yoga ball and a clip board. Inflate the ball so there's a slight dip for sitting.

The ball can be used for exercise to calm a child down.

When homework time comes, use the ball as a chair at a desk or put a worksheet on the clip board (pencil/pen attached) and allow the child sit on the ball with the clip board to work.

Additionally, walking around or moving on the ball helps some ADHD children focus.

~Kathleen R. Marikar, ADHD Coach

Kathleen Marikar, ADHD Coach Central, MA (978) 212-5855

If the Shoe Doesn't Fit, Don't Blame the Foot

One of the problems with ADHD is it's a bit like being left-handed in a right-handed world. People with ADHD are often hard on themselves because they can't do things the "right" way, not taking into account that, like lefties, their brains are just wired differently. If you feel frustrated because you can't stay organized using the systems everyone else uses, just remember, if the shoe doesn't fit, don't blame the foot! Find a strategy that does fit with how you naturally do things, and you will be a lot happier.

(With thanks to Madelyn Griffith-Haynie.)

~Sarah D. Wright, M.S., A.C.T.

Sarah D. Wright, M.S., A.C.T., internationally-known ADHD coach, speaker, author, expert, and founding Board Member of the ADHD Coaches Organization. Contact Sarah at:
Sarah@FocusForEffectiveness.com

The Opposite of "No" is Not Necessarily "Yes"

Saying "no" can be difficult. There is the triple whammy: New projects capture our interest (especially if they take us away from a boring project or task), we think "I should" be able to do that too, and we want to keep the harmony, help out or please others. Don't say "yes" or "no." Instead, say something like, "That sounds terrific. Let me think about it and get back to you (after lunch, tomorrow, next week, etc.)."

NOTE: This also works when the idea you are thinking about is your own, and the person you are getting back to is yourself.

~Susan Lasky, ADHD Strategist

Susan Lasky is a Master ADHD Strategist and Productivity & Organization Coach, helping adults and older students to get things done and enjoy life! (914) 373-4787 www.SusanLasky.com Susan@SusanLasky.com

Why Is Brain-Based Coaching Critical?

ADHD impacts major life activities. That's too important to delay treatment and/or hiring a brain-based ADHD coach to achieve optimal functioning. Sudden questions, changes or stress in your days may create a prefrontal cortex lockup and a startle/boggle state which affects complex planning and appropriate social behavior: A coach can help you plan for this by having a safe 'delaying phrase' to say or safe 'place' to go. You can then excuse yourself for a moment to say your phrase, thereby creating time to regain your composure and formulate an appropriate response. If you consistently feel worse after coaching, it's not a good fit....look elsewhere.

~Glen Hogard, SCAC

Glen Hogard, SCAC, ACO Co-Founder. Serving students, academicians and creative entrepreneurs in the US and internationally via telephone since 1999. www.glenhogard.com www.worldADHD.com

How to Stop ADHD from Standing Between You and Your Partner

- Gain a thorough understanding of ADHD in order to help distinguish behaviors attributed to lack of love or understanding from veritable features of the disorder.
- Diminish criticism, as too much on the part of the non-ADHD partner could result in the couple falling into a parent-child relationship pattern, which would be detrimental to the relationship.
- Divide tasks between you to play to each partner's strengths.
- Break down tasks for the ADHD partner in order to avoid overwhelm.
- Try to have fun together as much as possible in order to nourish the relationship.

~Roya Kravetz, ADHD Coach

Roya Kravetz specializes in coaching youth and adults with ADHD, as well as educating and coaching parents regarding ADHD and/or related challenges. www.adhdsuccesscoaching.com (858) 334-8584

Chaos

I am convinced that the natural order of the world is "chaos." Unless we tend to it or maintain something, it will eventually return to this most basic state. People with ADHD often describe their lives as "chaotic," unsure how "other" people maintain otherwise. This is the trick. People who are organized have discovered, or naturally do, what most people with ADHD don't know. Daily and consistent attention keeps the chaos at bay and keeps their lives in order. It is not that they are better organizers; rather, they are more persistent and consistent with their attempts. So, set aside a few minutes every day. Maybe set a timer. Spend five minutes picking up your desk, sorting the mail, checking your "to-do list". It will help to put your world back in order.

~Laurie Dupar, PMHNP, RN, PCC

Laurie Dupar, PMHNP, Certified ADHD Coach, specializes in helping you understand your brain, navigate the treatment maze, reduce your challenges and get things done! www.CoachingforADHD.com

What Was That?

Following directions is a problem for many children with ADHD. They may appear to be listening but later are unable to do the required tasks! In fact, they can look directly at you while their minds are racing. These students miss steps, have incomplete work or engage in another unrelated activity! Try these to facilitate better attention skills:

1. Be brief when giving instructions.
2. Allow the child to do one step at a time.
3. If the child loses focus, gently redirect him/her.
4. Write the directions down or write in colors on a whiteboard.
5. Use a multi-modality approach (tactile, auditory and visual)!
6. Have the students repeat the instructions back to you!

~B-J Ray-Bertram, M.S.

B-J Ray-Bertram, M.S., Grade 3 Teacher, Reading Specialist

Easy Button

Many adults with ADD may be impulsive or lack filters, tending to say and do things without stopping to think about how it sounds, who it will hurt, or what the consequences will be. Instead of automatically saying or sending via email what is thought, I ask them to hit the pause button, which is much like the Staples Easy Button. Take a breath, re-read or re-think about what you are about to say or write before you say it. Stop, breath, and re-think: how would I feel if someone said this to me? Then say or send it.

~Deb Bollom, PCC, ACG

Deb Bollom, PCC, ACG, works with entrepreneurs and adults who hate details and feel overwhelmed to discover their strengths and create ways to move forward. www.d5coaching.com (715) 386-6860

Moving Up the Corporate Ladder? Tips for ADHDers on the Rise

1. Allow superiors to set the tone of the meeting. In telephone meetings, press mute after introductions.

2. Let the presenter shine. It is impolite to "show up" colleagues in this setting. You will appreciate this when it is your turn to speak.

3. Avoid interrupting; write down thoughts instead. This is essential for ADHDers who fear forgetting thoughts, or topics changing before they can speak. There will usually be a chance to ask permission to return to a topic later.

4. Acknowledge whoever speaks before you with a compliment or statement of understanding before speaking. Don't fear kissing up. We all like to be acknowledged.

5. Take slow, deep breaths to calm your mind.

~Linda Richmand, ADHD Coach

Linda Richmand, Business, Career, and Life Coach pecializing in adult AD/H/D, www.CoachRichmand.Com (914) 330-9103

How to Tell Someone that You are Tired of Being Told What to Do

If you find that a relative or friend feels the need to always tell you how to do things the "right way," or complains about HOW you do something, here are some suggestions for showing you are intelligent. You can ask, "What about what I do makes you feel the need to correct me?" Or, you can say, "If you truly want to help empower me, then I need you to explain each step, showing me how to do_____." Or, finally, you can say, "I may not do this the way you do it, but this works for me. Thank you for your input."

~Sandy Alletto Corbin, M.A., SCAC

Ms. Sandy Alletto Corbin, M.A., SCAC, Certified Senior ADHD Coach and Advocate working with families, teens and women. She can be reached at http://www.lifecoachsandyalletto.com

Pull Out of Overwhelm with Clarity

When feeling overwhelmed, your mind is whirling and everything is a blur. You need to get a very clear sense of what must be done, and when. Take one project at a time and write down every single step that must be done for that project and what actual tasks / activities you must perform. For each activity, visualize yourself doing it. Break it down further to its simplest task form, making sure each individual task is clear and NOT overwhelming. Create a checklist of all the tasks, with the earliest ones on top and any due dates marked in red.

~Bonnie Mincu, SCAC

Bonnie Mincu, Senior ADHD Coach and founder of "THRIVE with ADD," has numerous classes, tools and resources on Adult ADHD challenges at www.thrivewithadd.com. (914) 478-0071
bonnie@bonniemincu.com

"The fastest way to succeed is to look as if you're playing by somebody else's rules, while quietly playing by your own."

~Michael Konda

Does He Work as Hard to Keep Up with Me as I Do to Slow Down for Him?

If you're telling the story, do you jump between topics, confusing your listener? Sometimes telling the end of the story before you get into it can help you stay focused.

If a specific reaction is expected at the end—i.e. if you don't want advice—tell the listener what you expect at the start. I like to start the conversation saying, "Your response at the end of this story will be to say, 'Wow! What a jerk!' Now please repeat your line," obviously said with a giant smile! When I get to the end of the story, or if he starts to give advice, I say, "Here's where you say your line," making a big flourish with my arms to queue his part.

~Kerch McConlogue, PCC, CPCC

Kerch McConlogue, PCC, CPCC, works with adults in Baltimore and around the world who have ADHD. Find her on the web at www.mapthefuture.com

Teens, Is It Hard for You to RECALL Certain Things?

People are not consciously aware of most of the information they take in.

Do you have a hard time remembering instructions that were just given, forget to write down assignments, find it difficult to remember multi-step directions?

Strengthen your working memory. Improve your RECALL when you:

- Review your working memory problem.
- Establish desired outcome.
- Create memory aids: acronyms, sentences, acrostics, chunks, flash cards, links, etc.
- Allow time to practice skill or strategy.
- List steps of tasks or information in order.
- Link information together, two at a time, using mental pictures.

~Laurie Moore Skillings, SCAC

Laurie Moore Skillings, SCAC is an ADHD Teen Coach. She helps teens understand ADHD and how it can affect their lives.

A Magic Cure for ADHD?

Searching for a quick fix for living more easily with ADHD will only disappoint you.

Tough news, I know, but it's true.

No silver bullet or medication will make ADHD magically disappear.

Before your ADHD symptoms can change, YOU have to change.

Lasting ADHD success comes from adopting one new ADHD management technique or habit at a time and giving it a chance to work.

Don't totally abandon a new technique or habit that isn't immediately perfect. People with ADHD often make things too complicated. Perhaps a small, simple adjustment will do the trick.

~Dana Rayburn, SCAC

Dana Rayburn, Senior Certified ADHD Coach, helps adults outsmart their Attention Deficit and live more successful and satisfying lives. Read free articles at www.danarayburn.com

Horse Blinders in My Toolkit?

The ADHD mind is often filled with non-stop ideas and thoughts. Overwhelm and distraction can be reduced by using virtual or imaginary "blinders".

Customize your "blinders" by identifying what needs to be focused on solely right now.

Next, enhance the focus by adjusting your "tuners" like that of a television, increase color brightness and clarity, turn up the volume or enlarge the picture.

Similarly, decrease outside distractions or thoughts by turning the rest of your visual field black and white, muting or lowering the sound, and shrinking the excess view. This tool can be helpful for memory and studying.

~Melissa R. Fahrney, M.A., CPC

Melissa Fahrney, M.A., CPC ADHD/Stress Management Coach for kids, college students & adults www.ADDHeartWorks.com www.facebook.com/addheartworks "Don't stress out, master your mountain, with heart!" (888) 327-5727

Harness the Power of Hyperfocus

My ability to hyper-focus is a blessing. It got me an "A" in a college class I never went to and helped me go from an admin assistant to a global project manager in ten years. But like many with ADHD, I only saw the benefit and never acknowledged the price. And there is a price. Making the connection between hours of hyperfocus one day and a debilitating headache the next day was the key that changed my perspective. Now I can choose to leverage my hyperfocus ability when the need arises by consciously deciding if it's worth the price.

~Rori Boyce, ADHD Coach

Rori Boyce, ADHD Coach, Alton Bay, NH turningleafcoaching.com

Words Really Do Matter

Choose the words you use to describe yourself and your ADD challenges carefully! If your words are full of blame and shame, they are not helping you build upon or focus on your strengths! If you can take the blame and shame and accompanying moral judgments out of your own thoughts, you can start to use your great problem-solving skills and out-of-the-box thinking to come up with creative ways to address your challenges. When we shift our perspective away from blame and shame and toward problem-solving, we can start to rely on our strengths and improve our functioning and fulfillment.

~Lynne A. Edris, ACG

Woman with ADD, Mom to ADHD Teen, ADD Coach, CHADD Parent 2 Parent Trainer. All ADD, All the Time!

Pick Your Battles

To prevent you and your teen from always fighting with each other, decide what is really important for your child's success...and fight for that. Ask yourself if matching (or even clean) clothes really matter, or if not making their bed every day is the best indicator of their future success or happiness. Make sure you're fighting over the important things. It will be hard and may mean letting go of past ideas, but it will allow both of you to put energy into what is most important for their success. So pick your battles wisely and you're more likely to win the war.

~Anonymous

Adult ADHD Symptoms

Up until recently, it was thought that people outgrew ADHD. Diagnosing ADHD in adults is a fairly recent development. Because the challenges in adults with ADHD are often different than those for children, they can go undiagnosed. Following are some of the more common challenges for adults with ADHD:

- Difficulty finalizing projects
- Forgetful and/or losing or misplacing things
- Frequently missing appointments
- Easily distracted
- Difficulty concentrating on what others are saying to you
- Interrupts frequently
- Pattern of broken promises
- Internal sense of restlessness

For more info www.chadd.org or www.add.org.

~Laurie Dupar, PMHNP, RN, PCC

Laurie Dupar, PMHNP, Certified ADHD Coach, specializes in helping you understand your brain, navigate the treatment maze, reduce your challenges and get things done! www.CoachingforADHD.com

Could Food Intolerances Be Affecting Your Brain?

Restrictive diets are often recommended for people with ADHD and Autism, including avoidance of food dyes, preservatives and sugars. Food intolerances are as individual as human beings are; no two are alike and for some people, food intolerances can mimic ADHD symptoms. Digestive problems, fatigue, rashes, joint pains, and headaches, along with mood or attention problems, are clues that food intolerance may be involved. A brief 2-3 week trial of an elimination diet and monitoring symptoms might be revealing. Testing for delayed food sensitivities can be worthwhile in some cases.

~Dr. Susan Wilder

Dr. Susan Wilder, CEO of LifeScape Medical Associates and LifeScape Premier, expert in nutritional testing and interventions for mood/attention problems in adults and children. www.lifescapepremier.com (480) 860-5269

Be Patient with Your Partner

Forgiving yourself for the struggles you've had due to ADHD is important to moving forward. So is having forgiveness from your spouse or loved one. Be patient, as this may not be as easy for them. With ADHD, you're probably quick to forgive, but your partner may not be so swift.

ADHD can cause a lot of frustration in relationships and these frustrations may have grown deeper than you realized. Keep in mind that your partner has stuck with you this long not knowing about the ADHD. Be patient with them now as they come to understand more about ADHD and begin to accept that things can be different.

~David Sloan

David Sloan, 31 yrs old, recently diagnosed with ADD
Columbia, SC

When Your Planner Stops Working, Resparklize!

Have you ever wondered why a system or calendar worked for you for a while then just didn't help anymore? When a good reminder system or calendar stops working, it's often because it's become familiar and our brain stops seeing it anymore. No problem! The ADHD brain is wired for novelty, which can work in our favor. Be creative and resparklize your planner...you'll be good to go. Use color, change the alarm, or add stickers; anything to catch your brain's attention. "Hey, that's new! What's that?" Your system will work just fine again . . . for a while. Resparklize again and you won't have to start over with another new planner.

~Barbara Luther, MCC

Barbara Luther, Master ADHD Certified Coach, www.WindBeneathYourWings.com President, Professional Association of ADHD Coaches, www.PAACCoaches.org Director of Training, ADD Coach Academy, www.addca.com www.SoaringCoachesCircle.com St. Louis, MO, (573) 340-3559

Top Ten Ways to Manage Adult ADHD

1. **ADHD Coaching** for practical skills and self-awareness
2. **ADHD Medication** balances brain chemistry
3. **Cognitive Behavioral Therapy**
4. **ADHD Support Groups**
5. **Adequate Diet**
6. **Exercise** helps you focus and reduces stress
7. **Learning to Slow Down** and Stop so you don't crash
8. **Meditation** that involves one of the five senses vs. "empty your mind"
9. **Tutors or Educational Psychologists** that know ADHD
10. **Professional and Personal Help** such as professional organizers, bookkeepers, virtual assistants, secretarial help, and maids

~Pete Quily, ADHD Coach

Pete Quily, Adult ADHD Coach www.ADDCoach4u.com See full list at http://bit.ly/manageadhd

Standard Grocery Checklist

Compile – on a spreadsheet if you are the accounting type — a standard grocery list. Include the items you buy most and other items you might forget. Be as detailed as possible (i.e. 1% milk, low-sodium turkey from the deli). The list makes it easy to see what you need each week and helps to not forget essential items you might miss. The details allow someone else to do the shopping – so you can delegate this task. Change it up as your eating habits or preferences change.

~Karen Peak, CPA

Karen Peak - not your typical certified public accountant - runs a successful tax and bookkeeping practice in Northern California, helping entrepreneurial clients from coast to coast. www.karenpeakcpa.com

Think It...Don't Do It!

Just because you think of something doesn't mean you have to do it!

The clock says it's time to leave! Instead of stopping what you are doing you continue with the distraction: clear the counter, clean the closet, make a quick phone call, read, or any quick tasks that just pop into your head. Save these distractions until later.

- Keep pencil and paper in every room and jot down these distractions.
- Later, plan them on your calendar at a time that doesn't interfere with getting out the door on time.

Your self-esteem will greatly improve because you won't have to make excuses for being late.

~Joyce A. Kubik, ADHD Coach

Joyce Kubik, ADHD Coach, www.bridgetosuccess.net

To Do List

A to-do list is just that: A list of things you expect to do on a daily basis. It's not a wish list. Only put specific tasks on it that you truly expect to get done.

~Carrie Greene, Trainer

Carrie Greene, speaker, trainer, coach and author of *Chaos to Cash*. She helps entrepreneurs cut through the chaos, make decisions, stop spinning and make money. http://www.CarrieThru.com

Procrastination: 3 Sure-Fire Tips for Getting Unstuck

- Piles of paper
- Unpaid bills
- Mounds of laundry
- Overdue appointments

What do all of these have in common?

Procrastination: a common symptom of ADHD!

Why We Procrastinate:

1. We under or over-estimate the timeframe.
2. We don't know how to do it.
3. We don't have the proper materials at hand.

What You Can Do:

- Write your to-do list while asking:
  - How long will it take?
  - Do I know how to do this? (If not, get help!)
  - Do I have the supplies?

Try it! By analyzing the roadblocks, you will be able to move forward.

~Terry Matlen, MSW, ACSW

Terry Matlen, ACSW, a nationally-recognized authority specializing in women with ADHD, is the author of "Survival Tips for Women with ADHD" and founder of www.ADDconsults.com

Freeze your Omega-3s

Will fish oil make you smarter? Maybe, maybe not, but it has been shown to improve ADHD symptoms. So take some. How much? For adults: 2-3 grams, but there's a catch–you must read the back of the label. Add the amount of EPA to the amount of DHA listed for the total Omega-3 benefit. Got the fish oil burps? The capsules go rancid at room temperature so store them in the freezer and swallow them icy cold. By the time they thaw, they'll be past the point of causing stomach distress.

~Linda Roggli, PCC, CLC

Linda Roggli, PCC, CLC Professional Certified Coach, Author of *"Confessions of an ADDiva: midlife in the non-linear lane"* http://confessionsofanaddiva.net

What We ADHD Folks Do Best!

The thing we (or at least I and all of the ADHD folks I live with and know) do best is forget! The most constructive thing to do about that is to NOT beat myself up for it, but to come up with systems to help me remember better. Post-it notes are my best friend…I have them all over the mirror in my bathroom and all over my office. A file folder works too, with one side for "to do" post-its that I transfer to the other side as instant gratification when they are done!

~Dee Doochin, MLAS, PCC

Dee Doochin, MLAS, Professional Certified Coach, Certified Mentor Coach, Senior Certified ADHD Coach, wife, mother, grandmother, great-grandmother with ADHD, adventurer, lover of life! www.addupcoach.com

Ta Dah!!!

Every time we made a mistake, our tribe made us take a bow and call attention to ourselves. Initially, my brain thought, 'There's something really wrong with this picture!' Fast forward 4 years, and I find myself focusing much of my practice on helping clients and their parents rewrite the definition of failure. Actually... is there failure? Or is it a perspective or attitude than can shift as we divert our thought pattern? Is there a learning? Is there growth? And how about an opportunity to begin again? Then... TA DAH, HURRAY, Que viva!! I'll take a long bow for that!

~Ana Isabel Sánchez, ADHD Life Coach

Ana Sánchez, sassy,authentic & witty mom, wife, Certified ADHD LifeCoach, friend, lawyer, passionate explorer of strengths. Curious about possibilities from 'I'm Able' stance.

Strategies to Improve Communication

1. Ask as many questions as you answer in a conversation.
2. Prep yourself before a social event by recalling names of people who may be there and come armed with a couple of topics that you could ask them about.
3. When talking on the phone, take notes; it will help you stay focused on the conversation.
4. If you didn't hear what someone said, it is okay to ask them to repeat it.
5. Look someone in the eye when you are talking to them.
6. Count to ten before you jump into a conversation. Use this time to learn what the topic is so you can participate.

Remember, most people just want to feel like you are listening. Knowing their name, asking them questions, allowing them to talk is the fastest way to social success!

~Laurie Dupar, PMHNP, RN, PCC

Laurie Dupar, Certified ADHD Coach, specializes in helping you understand your brain, navigate the treatment maze, reduce your challenges and get things done! www.CoachingforADHD.com

You Want Me to Say WHAT?

Yes, I'm suggesting you start your questions with the word WHAT.

When people hear HOW and WHY questions, they often feel confused or become defensive. This is especially true with people that have AD(H)D. They tend to internalize these questions and turn them into communication obstacles.

Using "WHAT" keeps the conversation focused on the subject matter and supports a more relaxed, open and honest answer. This works in school, business and life. “What was the test like? What was challenging? What do you like about sales? What do you need more of? What did you like about this tip?”

~Kricket Harrison, Motivational Speaker

Kricket Harrison, Professional Coach and Motivational Speaker, is an expert at maximizing creative potential and developing strategies for success based on individual learning styles. www.BrightOutsidetheBox.com

"It is never too late to become who you might have been."

~George Eliot

Turning TO DO into Ta Dah!

- Be realistic about what you can accomplish in one day.
- Break down projects into do-able steps, choosing one task to start with.
- Experiment to see how you work most effectively: Do you need to do the easiest things first to gain momentum or start with the hardest tasks so they get done? Do you work best when you finish one task before starting another, or when you alternate tasks? What kinds of breaks work best?
- Be proactive about things that are important to you...motivation follows.
- Review your day and celebrate your successes.

~Roxanne Fouche, ADHD Coach

Roxanne Fouche, ADHD Coach and Consultant, specializes in working with individuals of all ages with ADHD and LD and related challenges www.FocusForEffectiveness.com/blog
Roxanne@RoxanneFouche.com (858) 484-4749

Can't Find the Right Word?

One of my clients came up with a solution if she gets stuck when writing. She justs starts typing random words that come to mind. Eventually she finds the right word. She calls this her "hunt for gold."

~Laurie Senders, PhD.

My son's early diagnosis and my own diagnosis started my journey to slay the dragons of ADHD. I coach motivated ADHD adults. www.compellingADHDcoach.com

Get Big Things Done, Just Start a Small Habit.

The power of the small is the secret to building great things. Is there a project/ skill/ routine that you haven't been able to achieve? Think small.

Spend 20 minutes each and every day, without exception, working on some aspect of your goal and it will become a habit. In a month, you will feel restless and incomplete if you haven't engaged in your small step activity yet that day.

Don't be surprised if your daily work allotment increases, but always be sure to meet your "minimum daily requirement." A coach or accountability partner can help ensure success with this!

~Susan Bright Nguyen, ADHD Coach

Susan Bright Nguyen, Certified ADHD Coach, www.waytogocoaching.net I help talented and motivated individuals with ADD achieve their personal and career goals.

Don't Be a Personality Contortionist

Banish "should" from your vocabulary. This word undermines the talents, skills, abilities, qualities, quirks, and true uniqueness of yourself and other people. She *should* be a faster runner. He *should* make more money. I *should* be thinner, kinder, less picky, more open, and less scattered. Should sends the message that what you ARE doing and who you ARE isn't enough. But it is, and you are. Ban "should." Stop trying to be good at everything. Refuse to become a personality contortionist. Don't bend and break and pour yourself into someone else's mold. Be you, not who someone thinks you should be.

~Rori Boyce, ADHD Coach

Rori Boyce, ADHD Coach, Alton Bay, NH Turningleafcoaching.com

To Tell or Not?

You do not necessarily have to tell about your diagnosis/diagnoses at work; instead, you can start telling people what works best for you!

~Marie Enback, ADHD Coach

Marie Enback is the first ADHD Coach in Sweden, initiator of ADHD Awareness Week Sweden, conference organizer, writer, speaker and educator. www.adhdcoaching.se www.lateralia.se www.adhdawarenessweek.se

FAB FIVE & FINAL FOUR

Build a sequence to teach your child routines.

FAB FIVE is our morning start-up routine:

1. Get dressed
2. Eat breakfast
3. Take medications
4. Grooming (teeth, hair, etc.)
5. Gather the day's stuff at door (backpack, keys, etc.)

FINAL FOUR is for night time:

1. Grooming (bath/shower, teeth, etc)
2. Dressed for bed
3. Wind down
4. Prayers and good nights

~Robin Nordmeyer, ADHD Coach

ADHD Coach, Robin Nordmeyer, www.LifeAheadCoaching.com

Strategies for Acing College

The excitement of heading off to college is often mixed with the hope that academic challenges will be met. Here are some success strategies for college gathered from previous clients:

- Always go to class. Skipping once or twice is a slippery slope to not going at all.
- Get to know other students in your class. When someone is expecting you, it helps give you incentive to show up and meet your study partners.
- Get to know your professor. Make a point of introducing yourself to your instructor. Sign up for help during their office hours.
- Know the student services options at your college even if you don't plan to use them.

~Laurie Dupar, PMHNP, RN, PCC

Laurie Dupar, PMHNP, RN, Certified ADHD Coach
www.CoachingforADHD.com

Put Disorganization in Perspective

"Disorganization is merely a problem to be solved. It's not a character flaw."

Now, there's a statement that always hits home with my clients who are chronically disorganized and/or have ADHD.

When you accept this truth, you open the door for improved self-esteem, happiness, peace—and problem-solving!

~Debbie Stanley, LLPC, NCC, CPO-CD

Debbie Stanley is a licensed mental health counselor specializing in chronic disorganization and hoarding, both of which often co-occur with ADHD. www.thoughtsinorder.com

A Rocket Needs Guidance and Space – not Gravity!

People can be somewhat tolerant of other ADHD symptoms, but yet be unforgiving about the behavior of the hyperactive child with ADHD. Research shows that hyperactive ADHD children are not willfully trying to be disruptive – they have a real need for activity. Provide channels for their hyperactivity like the use of a rocking chair while reading. Give opportunities to release energy throughout their day; recess is a solution and not an opportunity for punishment. Allow for movement with classroom chores and structure the transitions between active and deskbound events. The effort is worth it, because this child is worth it.

~Katherine B. Jahnke

Those with ADHD deserve the same fabulous life as anyone. My coaching emphasizes doing and being what we love, and what's holding us back.

Take Green Breaks

It has been proven that spending time with Nature decreases stress. As we know, reduction in stress increases our ability to create attention. So, adding a few 'Green Breaks' to your day has multiple benefits. These breaks can be as extravagant as going for a long walk through an arboretum or as simple as spending a few moments paying attention to an indoor plant. The key is, be there completely with the Nature in front of you. Breathe it in, take it in fully, and it will create a shift.

~Ian King, Speaker

Ian King, Coach/Speaker specializing in ADHD and gifted adults, children, families, and entrepreneurs. Past President of ADHD Coaches Organization & ICF Chicago. www.KingSolutionsInc.com

Managing Time for College Coeds

Managing your time wisely in college leads to higher grades and less stress. Use these tips to help you organize your time:

- Use daily/weekly planners, either paper or computer-based.
- Put dates from the semester calendar & class syllabi into calendar and planner and set reminders.
- Schedule a time for daily planning (takes 5 minutes).
- Block out specific study times; keep them the same each week.
- Use alarms on your phone to alert you to head to class, start studying, take medication, get to appointments, get ready for bed, turn off the computer, and more.

~Casey Dixon, MSEd, CTACC

Casey Dixon, MSEd, CTACC. www.dixonlifecoaching.com

The Best Use of Your Time

Ask yourself, "How much time each week do I spend with people who can really see me and value me?" and "How much time each week do I spend doing things I am really good at or enjoy?" This is how you develop feelings of competency and connection. Simple Advice:

> *Find people who value you. Spend as much time with them as possible.*
>
> *Find something to do that you are good at. Spend as much time doing it as possible.*

Get support for the tasks you aren't as good at and that drain you of vital mental and physical energy.

~Sari Solden

Sari Solden, a psychotherapist in Ann Arbor, MI, has worked with adults with ADHD for 23 years and is a national speaker and the author of *Women with ADD* and *Journeys Through ADDulthood.* ADDJourneys.com sari@sarisolden.com

My Favorite Nuggets

GETTING THINGS DONE: Think like a waiter or waitress - As you walk through your house or workspace, pick up what you can and put it away – you don't need to wait for when you are "cleaning."

SHORTCUTS: Create pre-made lists for such chores as grocery shopping and packing for trips so that you don't have to generate a list each time.

TIME MANAGEMENT: When putting a task in your calendar, include the time it takes to transition, such as getting materials ready and traveling from one appointment to the next.

~Debbie Tracht, M.A., ACAC

Debbie Tracht, M.A., ACAC, Certified ADHD Coach for College Students, Adults with ADHD and Parents of Children with ADHD. debbie@focusresourcecenter.com (802) 349-7222

ADHD: 'A' is for Anxiety

Most people with ADHD will, at some point, suffer from anxiety that is stronger or more persistent than normal. Many will have physical issues: insomnia, digestive problems, aches, and other symptoms associated with "stress." Here's what helps:

- Exercise
- Mindful meditation
- Getting away from the news and electronics
- Puzzles
- Improved diet
- Improved sleep habits
- Supportive relationships

If these lifestyle options aren't possible or don't help, see a specialist. Anxiety is treatable and it's worth the effort to get it under control so you can get on with your life. For more information, go to www.FocusForEffectiveness.com/blog.

~Sarah D. Wright, M.S., A.C.T.

Sarah D. Wright, M.S., A.C.T., internationally-known ADHD coach, speaker, author, and expert. Founding Board Member of the ADHD Coaches Organization. Sarah@FocusForEffectiveness.com

7 Reasons to Get an ADHD Coach*

1. ADHD coaching is like athletic coaching, only they help you be a more rounded/better "player" in the game of life.

2. Your coach helps you change things you want to change.

3. ADHD coaches really understand what you are going through. They may even have ADHD themselves.

4. An ADHD coach helps you understand your ADHD strengths.

5. What you work on with your coach will help you better manage your ADHD now and in the future.

6. Your coach knows you are more than just your ADHD.

7. Your ADHD coach can help you figure out how to "do" things in ways that work best for you and your ADHD brain style.

8. Your coach helps you follow through on what you want to accomplish by providing consistent support and accountability.

*Adapted from The Edge www.EdgeFoundation.org

Teen Tip: Feeling Scattered? Create a System.

Organizing is the ability to create and maintain ways to keep track of information or materials. It's a process that can be learned.

Remember, organization is a personal thing. Whatever you are organizing needs to be set up to work for you, not for someone else. Here are some ideas:

- Create and use systems that are as simple as you need them to be.
- Simplify the task.
- You need to (help) create the system. Specify the function of the system.
- Target zones: electronics, books, clothing, etc. Establish checklists for each zone.
- Monitor/modify the system as needed.

~Laurie Moore Skillings, SCAC

Laurie Moore Skillings, Senior Certified ADHD Coach, specializing in working with teens that have a hard time with school. Laurie can be reached at: laurie@addwithease.com

The Big Picture

When you're having a hard time finding a good solution to a particular challenge, try this exercise. Place a chair physically in front of you. The chair is your obstacle. Give your obstacle a name (example: money). Stand up against it. It's hard to see how to get around it. Take two or three steps back. Do you see all your options now? You can go around it, crawl under it, climb over it, or move it. Apply this to your real challenge. You could cut spending, earn more, save more. Stepping back and looking at the big picture is the key.

~Dr. Billi, Ph.D.

The AttentionB Method, Pedagogical/Class Management for ADHD with Dr. Billi, Ph.D. Tame the Chaos in your Classroom Using my Unique Strategies. www.AttentionB.com, DrBilli@AttentionB.com, (855) Dr Billi

Organization

As an adult with ADHD, you face the challenge of managing various roles in life. Becoming organized is a great way to make sense of your numerous responsibilities. Try the following easy steps:

- Create three folders that you keep at your side.
- Label them:
  1. Mail and correspondence
  2. Reading, Projects
  3. Miscellaneous
- Clear your work area of all items.
- Collect the items requiring your attention and place those into groups.
- Examine each group and decide what needs to be done with it.
- Remember that everything belongs in a specific place (determine what that is for you.)
- Strive to stay organized each day.

~Dulce Torres, LPC-S, ADHD Coach

Dulce Torres, LPC-S, ADHDCoach: Coaching helps individuals to discover their own possibilities and strengths.
Bilingual Services available (817) 707-6264
www.dstcoaching.com dtorres@dstcoaching.com

The Calendar

I have to use Outlook synched to my smart phone to keep track of meetings and commitments. I make sure I set reminders so I don't miss something. Early on, I learned that Outlook didn't help much if I wasn't at my computer to be reminded, so I first bought a Palm Pilot in 1997. Now with my smart phone, when I'm away from my desk and get distracted in conversations, etc., my smart phone is with me to taser me back on track. I also check it before bed so I don't miss an early-morning meeting.

~Anonymous

Top 15 Tips for Parents

1. Educate yourself about ADHD.
2. Separate ADHD-related behaviors from non-ADHD-related ones.
3. Acknowledge your child's strengths.
4. Advocate for your child.
5. Avoid power struggles.
6. Focus on your child's successes without comparing him/her to others.
7. Choose your battles.
8. Follow through with logical consequences.
9. Point out the positive characteristics of ADHD (e.g., being an "out of the box" thinker).
10. Offer choices.
11. Work together on having smooth mornings.
12. Be firm and loving.
13. Spend quality time together.
14. Set clear limits and stick to them.
15. Vow to stop nagging or yelling.

~Roya Kravetz, ADHD Coach

Roya Kravetz specializes in coaching youth and adults with ADHD, as well as educating and coaching parents regarding ADHD and/or related challenges. roya@adhdsuccesscoaching.com (858) 334-8584

Test for Nutritional Deficiencies Before Conception if Possible

We often find similar patterns of nutrient deficiencies when testing mothers and children with ADHD. While there could be many reasons for this correlation, including similar diets, environments, and genetics, it raises the possibility that growing a baby in a nutritionally-depleted environment might impact healthy brain development. While this warrants extensive research before we can make any conclusions about preventing ADHD, it makes sense that being in optimal nutritional health is critical to our most important life process: producing a healthy baby.

~Dr. Susan Wilder

Dr. Susan Wilder, CEO of LifeScape Medical Associates and LifeScape Premier, is an expert in nutritional testing and interventions for mood/attention problems in adults and children. www.lifescapepremier.com (480) 860-5269

The Many Faces of ADHD

One of the difficulties of diagnosing ADHD, and why I think many people are not diagnosed until adulthood, is because ADHD has so many different characteristics. Of course, in order to be diagnosed with ADHD, people must meet the criteria of inattention, hyperactivity or impulsivity. But often, it is not that obvious. A useful analogy of how different ADHD can "look," be experienced, or effect different people is to think of the face. We all have eyes, a nose and a mouth. However, how these features blend together make us uniquely different from anyone else. It's the same with ADHD. What does your ADHD look like?

~Laurie Dupar, PMHNP, RN, PCC

Laurie Dupar, PMHNP, Certified ADHD Coach, specializes in helping you understand your brain, navigate the treatment maze, reduce your challenges and get things done! www.CoachingforADHD.com

The Power of Curiosity

Be curious. Open yourself up to the adjustments you can make when you view your challenges with curiosity, not judgment.

Spend some time each day noticing: what IS working for you? What is not? When you observe that something is not working, ask yourself, "What if?" or "What other possibilities are available to me?" and then try them.

Experiment and play with other approaches beyond your usual menu of options. Then notice again, what IS working for you? What is not? Remain curious.

~Christina Fabrey, ADHD Coach

Christina Fabrey is a certified Life and ADHD Coach specializing in transition to college and college students. www.christinafabrey.com cfabrey@gmail.com (802) 345-2046

"The secret to productive goal setting is establishing clearly defined goals, writing them down and then focusing on them several times a day with words and emotions as if we've already achieved them."

~Denis Waitley

Get a Coach!

An ADHD coach can help you set goals, plan strategies and develop routines so that you can stay on top of things.

An ADHD coach can help you tackle the key Executive Functioning Skills: working memory; organization and planning; self-monitoring and emotional control; moving from one focus to another; initiating tasks; and organizing materials.

I know from experience that coaching will help you live a better life by defining your goals and working to achieve those goals. But just be sure you find someone trained in ADHD coaching!

~Abigail Wurf, M.Ed

ADHD Coach Abigail Wurf, M.Ed My life experience/training makes me confident that together, we can make a positive difference in your life! www.abigailwurf.com www.awurf@verizon.net
(202) 244-2234

"Rise and Shine" Affirmations

Negative self talk, those mean negative voices in my head. They can make or break my day, immobilize me so that I get nothing done. Did you ever pay attention to the first thought you have when you first awaken? Here are a few examples of what my negative voice says to me when I arise..I am still tired, I have too much to do, it's too hot, I am so fat, I hate laundry, what a slob! This is the a.m. ritual I do to feel good about who I am, which energizes my spirit to move forward: Before I get out of bed, I say out loud positive affirmations and/or what I am grateful for!

~Sheryl Greenfield, ADHD Coach

Sheryl Greenfield, ADHD Coach, Coaching adults, teens and college kids, Bryn Mawr, PA. www.ADHDADULTCOACHING.com Focusonnewbeginnings@aol.com (610) 812-9546

Parenting a Child Who has ADHD?

Hold this in your heart:

They don't mean to frustrate you. They don't want to make life so challenging and difficult, for you or for themselves.

Just as some children have trouble learning how to read, children with ADHD often have trouble tolerating frustration, being flexible, and solving their problems independently. Like learning to decode words, these, too, are skills your child needs to learn and develop.

Rewards and punishments can't teach skills – but you can. It may take incredible patience, understanding, investigation, perseverance, and learning on your part – but it's worth it!

Parent the child you have!

~Cindy Goldrich, Ed. M., ACAC

Cindy Goldrich, Ed. M., ACAC, Certified ADHD Parent Coach
www.PTScoaching.com Cindy@PTScoaching.com
(516) 802-0593 Coaching available in New York and Telephone.
Parent the Child YOU have!

Preventing Failure in College with ADHD

Making informed choices with a plan needs to be a partnership between parent and teen. Knowing the facts of your life with ADD is critical to self-advocate in obtaining services via the Disability Office and the College Learning Center. Learn all you can about ADD and what your rights are. Asking for help is virtuous; suffering in silence is sabotage. Devise a system to stay on track with self-imposed rules, as well as a prioritized, structured daily routine. Withdraw from a class in a timely way if it overwhelms you, rendering you academically paralyzed and sending your progress plummeting in all classes.

~Fran Parker, Ph.D.

For the past 13 years, Dr Fran Parker has specialized in treating college students and families with ADHD. She is an instructor for CHADD's Parenting Program and the recipient of a Leadership Award in 2010.

Guidelines for Successful Parenting

- Love abundantly
- Discipline constructively
- Spend time with your children
- Give the needs of your mate a priority
- Teach your children right from wrong
- Develop mutual respect
- Listen
- Foster independence
- Be realistic
- Expect mistakes

~Anonymous

10 Reasons I love my ADHD

1. I always win at Trivia.
2. I never get bored.
3. I always laugh at my husband's jokes like it is the first time that I heard them.
4. I easily forget what made me mad 10 minutes ago.
5. I always know where to find my shoes.... because people are always tripping over them.
6. I love my eclectic group of friends.
7. I know a little about a lot.
8. I have learned that Costco sells reading glasses in bulk.
9. I find money in my pockets.
10. I know how to laugh at myself.

~Jo Ann Skinner, ACAC

Jo Ann Skinner, ACAC, Certified ADHD Coach in Reston, VA.
Jo Ann coaches and advocates for students and adults with ADHD.
www.joannskinner.com joannsskinner@yahoo.com (703) 925-0510

Pursue Your Passions

Doing anything you "love" stimulates or increases natural Dopamine. It's the brain's neurochemical needed for focus, concentration, good memory, prioritizing, organizing, and decision-making, among many other important abilities. If you have to do something tedious, boring or mentally challenging, try to do something "fun" first or alternate throughout the task to “rev up” or maintain your Dopamine levels. You'll get things done more quickly and accurately.

Ideally, you will find the right career or academic courses that you love.

Each day, always incorporate some of your "passions" into your life and schedule. It's a must for someone with ADHD!

~Victoria Ball, M.ED, MCC, SCAC

Victoria Ball, ADD Career Coach, specializes in identifying successful college/career choices and life/work/productivity strategies. www.ADDventuresinliving.com (401) 272-0435

A Record with Two Sides

Visualize an old record. Now picture the needle getting stuck on one song. This is often what happens to people with ADHD, and it leads to impulsivity.

A tip to slow down a rash decision would be to visualize side A of a record album, containing all of the great reasons to buy or do something right now—the fun stuff—just like side A of the record. Now flip the record to slow down the impulsive feelings and look at side B, the consequences to a quick decision.

After pausing to look at both sides of the record, make a great decision!

~Melissa M. Rutherford

Melissa M. Rutherford, ADD/HD Expert & Life Coach, Tulsa, OK
www.melissacoaching.com

Three Valuable Time Tips

1. Out of sight, out of mind. Keep your calendar visible!

2. Do you hide things from yourself?

   Everything you use on a daily basis needs a home base where you can see it. This will save precious time and lower anxiety ...unless you thrive on raising your blood pressure looking for things.

3. Do you have a big project that needs starting?

   Picture it finished and then run a "video" backwards in your mind, imagining the steps needed for completion. Then you can make cartoons of the steps on sticky notes.

~Laurie Senders, Ph.D.

Laurie Senders, Ph.D. www.compellingADHDcoach.com

"Something to Live By"

If you feel "BLAH" or unmotivated, read this quote. I have been reading it for over 40 years! From "Something to Live By" (1945) by Dorothea S. Kopplin:

"The Victor" by, C. W. Longenecker
If you think you are beaten, you are;
If you think you dare not, you don't.
If you'd like to win, but think you can't,
It's almost a cinch you won't.
If you think you'll lose, you're lost,
For out in the world we find
Success begins with a fellow's will;
It's all in the state of mind.
Life's battles don't always go
To the stronger or faster man;
But sooner or later, the man who wins
Is the one who thinks he can.

~Cindy Giardina, PCC

Contact Cindy Giardina, PCC, with your favorite inspiring quote. cindy@kaleidoscope-coaching.com (973) 694-5077

**In Honor and Memory of A. Rocco Capobianco, Thanks, Dad, for "Something to Live By"*

End Procrastination: Seven Steps to Success

Procrastination is the avoidance of a task that needs to be done and can lead to feelings of guilt, depression and self-doubt. Put into action the seven steps below to end procrastination forever!

1. Make a list of everything you have to do. What seems overwhelming in our head almost always fits onto a piece of paper.
2. If you can't answer why a task is important for you to do, take it off your list.
3. Now set realistic goals of what you really want to get done. Remember, there are only 24 hours in a day and 7 days in a week.
4. Break tasks down into steps or pieces.
5. Ask yourself how long it will take to complete each step.
6. Multiply the above answer by two to get a more realistic time frame.
7. Then reward yourself when you get things done!

~Laurie Dupar, PMHNP, RN, PCC

Laurie Dupar, Nurse Practitioner, Certified ADHD Coach, specializes in helping you understand your brain, navigate the treatment maze, reduce your challenges and get things done! www.CoachingforADHD.com Laurie@coachingforadhd.com

Say "Yes" to Yourself

Learning how to say "No!" to too much stuff in our lives and our calendars is an important part of learning to live from your strengths. If something doesn't bring you joy and move you forward, it likely will bring more clutter to your life—eventually causing you more guilt and shame. So, how do you say "No"? A good place to start is to never say "Yes" on the spot! Take time to check your calendar, check with your partner, and think it through. Make sure you can afford to take on the new commitment without short-changing yourself or others.

~Lynne A. Edris, ACG

Lynne A. Edris, ACG, Life & ADHD Coach, CHADD Parent 2 Parent Trainer, ADD Coach for Dr. Kenny Handelman at Attention Difference Insiders www.CoachingADDvantages.com (717) 877-9853

Time Everything!

If you know exactly how long it takes to empty the dishwasher, you might get a kid to do that 3-minute job during a commercial! Or you might get it nearly done while waiting for a cup of coffee to heat up!

How long does it take to walk the dog? Sweep the kitchen floor? Time those annoying small jobs.

They aren't so bad if you know how long it actually takes to do them.

Start the timer. Look at it at the end. If you forgot this time, there WILL be another chance.

~Kerch McConlogue, PCC, CPCC

Kerch McConlogue kerch@mapthefuture.com (410) 929-3274

Gratitude

I have discovered that the best way to end my day is with a gratitude list. I simply jot down three things I'm grateful for in a notebook I keep by my bed. I don't have to list "big" things; in fact, I've found when I list the "little" things, they mean the most and make the biggest impact. By ending my day with a sense of gratitude, it is easier to begin the next day the same way. Before getting out of bed, I think of three things I am looking forward to and grateful for.

~Dee Doochin, MLAS

Dee Doochin, MLAS, Professional Certified Coach, Certified Mentor Coach, Senior Certified ADHD Coach, wife, mother, grandmother, great-grandmother with ADHD, adventurer, lover of life! www.addupcoach.com

Build Lifelong Habits with Weekly Family Meetings

Here's a great way to model planning skills and get everyone in the family on the same page for the week ahead!

Set a standing meeting time each Sunday and ask everyone to come to the table with their school planners.

Then take turns sharing the week's important upcoming dates: dad's birthday, a dentist appointment or that long-term school project.

Ask questions to get kids thinking ahead – do they need poster paper for that project? What mini deadlines will they set for themselves?

If your children take medicine, this is a perfect time to piggyback another great habit ~ filling their weekly pill organizers under your supervision.

~Becky Wheeler, ADHD Coach

Rebecca C. Wheeler, ADHD & Life Coach, New Focus Coaching, LLC, Alexandria, VA Structure * Skills * Strategy * Support. bwheeler@newfocuscoach.com (703) 980-0809

When ADHD is the Culprit – Become the Detective!

When you have ADHD, it is often challenging to do things others seem to find so simple, such as keeping the house neat, arriving for appointments on time (or remembering them), handing in homework you worked so hard to finish, etc…

Others think we don't really care, but usually we care too much; we become frustrated and overly critical of our performance (or lack thereof). We question our abilities and label ourselves failures.

Instead, keep it positive - "My ADHD got in the way, but I'll put on my detective hat and discover effective strategies to keep ADHD out of my way."

~Susan Karyn Lasky, MA, SCAC

Susan Lasky is a Master ADHD Strategist, Productivity & Organization Coach, helping adults and older students to get things done and enjoy life! Susan@SusanLasky.com (914) 373-4787

Organize Receipts for Tax Time

We all know we should save receipts for tax purposes, but it can be tedious and overwhelming. But not having receipts come April can prove costly. An easy solution is to buy an accordion file with 10 or so tabs on top. Label each tab with tax categories: Charity, Paystubs, Business Expenses, etc. If you have a small business you can modify the categories to include meals, travel, vehicle, office supplies, telephone, etc. As you accumulate receipts, pop them into your accordion file in the appropriate category. At tax time, make a total of each category, and voila! You are done.

~Karen Peak, CPA

Karen Peak - not your typical certified public accountant - runs a successful tax and bookkeeping practice in Northern California, helping entrepreneurial clients from coast to coast. www.karenpeakcpa.com

Teen Tip: Do You Act Before You Think?

Practice SELF CONTROL.

Specify what impulsive behavior will be addressed.

- Establish when the impulsive behavior happens.
- List the desired behavior.
- Find ways the teen can display the desired behavior.
- Cue teen when the desired behavior is expected.
- Offer a variety of cues to choose from (verbal, nonverbal).

Natural consequences can be positive or negative.

- Try a new strategy ahead of time.
- Regularly practice that strategy.
- Observe how the teen did with the strategy.
- Listen to how the teen felt they did.

~Laurie Moore Skillings, SCAC

Laurie Moore Skillings, Senior Certified ADHD Coach, specializing in working with teens that have a hard time with school. Laurie can be reached at laurie@addwithease.com

Who is Holding You Accountable?

Find an accountability partner to help implement strategies that will help you succeed with ADHD. An accountability partner can be anyone who helps you stay on track after deciding which strategies to implement. Your partner should be someone who:

- Will hold you accountable
- Is not emotionally attached to your outcomes
- Will encourage you
- You trust explicitly
- Will not judge you
- Will talk with you regularly

ADHD coaches are excellent accountability partners, and they can help with setting goals and developing strategies.

Recent research confirms that coaching can improve self-confidence, organizational skills, time management and other skills.

~Laura Rolands, ADHD Coach

Laura Rolands is an Attention and ADHD Coach who helps students and adults pay attention and increase productivity. Connect with Laura at www.MyAttentionCoach.com

Decrease Your Test Anxiety

- Be prepared! Start studying at least two nights before the exam.
- Get a good night's sleep.
- View the exam as a chance to show what you know.
- Be well fueled; take fresh fruits, vegetables, or raw nuts to munch on.
- Be on time for the test.
- Read directions carefully, twice. Underline key directions to refer back to.
- Shift positions to help you relax.
- If you don't know the answer to a question, skip it and come back to it later.
- Be sure to BREATHE!

~Anonymous

Six Quick Tips

1. Designate a spot for everything so everything has its own clear space.
2. Use a "body double" (someone to keep you company and on task). This presence "obligates" you to get something done.
3. Make simple task lists.
4. Create standard lists of repeated activities that you have trouble remembering.
5. Hire or trade out things you can't or just won't do. For example, hire someone twice a month to pay your bills and do your filing.
6. Use a calendar of some sort relentlessly. Check it multiple times a day.

~Abigail Wurf, M.Ed.

ADHD Coach Abigail Wurf, M.Ed My life experience/training makes me confident that together, we can make a positive difference in your life! www.abigailwurf.com www.awurf@verizon.net
(202) 244-2234

Why Would a Child with ADHD Need Speech Therapy?

Many children who have ADHD struggle in three areas of speech and language development: vocabulary, pragmatics (social language) and working memory.

To improve my students' skills, I use thematic lessons related to the core curriculum that enables them to grasp new vocabulary at a faster rate. These thematic units contain social skills lessons including turn-taking, sharing, feelings and empathy.

Strategies to improve working memory include learning concepts first, next and last, following multi-step commands and repeating directions over and over to themselves so that they can remember the steps.

For effective results, speech therapy is part of a team approach with all professionals targeting the same goals.

~Lisa-Anne Ray-Byers

Lisa-Anne Ray-Byers, Speech-Language Pathologist, Author, Columnist www.AskLisaAnne.com

Family Finances

When one partner has ADD/ADHD, difficulties with financial management, impulsive spending, or the inability to hold a job can have a negative impact on family life.

But all is not lost!

Work to your strengths, accept help, and keep your family financially safe:

- Communicate with your partner and be honest.
- Determine a realistic weekly budget and stick to it.
- Withdraw your weekly budget in cash.
- Set up automatic withdrawal for bills.
- Keep no more than one credit card.
- Cap your credit card at a low limit and pay in full every month.

~Rose Steele, RN, PhD

Rose Steele, RN, PhD www.AdultADDCoaching.ca

Motivating Yourself

Berating yourself and shaming yourself are not good motivators. Move in the direction of your dreams and meaning instead. Don't spend your life and time waiting to get over your problems or trying to get rid of who you are. Instead of only focusing on your challenges, expand your self-picture to include *all* of you: your strengths, values, interests, and personal characteristics like warmth, curiosity, creativity, or humor.

~Sari Solden

Sari Solden, a psychotherapist in Ann Arbor, MI, has worked with adults with ADHD for 23 years and is a national speaker and the author of *Women with ADD* and *Journeys Through ADDulthood.* ADDJourneys.com sari@sarisolden.com

"Climb the stairway to the stars one step at a time."

~Anonymous

The Blame and Shame Game

It's very natural that shame and blame affect the dynamics between parents and children with ADHD. But parents can't perform at their best this way. It results in kids feeling guilty or ashamed, since children with ADHD are very emotionally sensitive. Teach your child that ADHD is not his/her fault. It's nothing to be ashamed of. Find a coach who can give you strategies to get over the blame/shame mindset, and practice them. I use psychodrama and other expressive art therapies, along with coaching, to help control emotions. Your attitude will eventually change. It's your choice how you want to live: with guilt or shame, or celebrating your family's uniqueness.

~Dr. Billi, Ph.D.

The AttentionB Method, Neuro-Cognitive Behavioral Therapy/Coaching with Dr. Billi, Ph.D. Let's Leap Toward a Brighter Future Together. Schedule a Coaching Session Now. www.AttentionB.com DrBilli@AttentionB.com (855) DrBilli

ADHD & Sleep

ADHD patients have difficulty initiating sleep. We're told to avoid caffeine at night because it will keep us up.

In reality, for many hyperactive (not inattentive) ADHD'ers, stimulants at night may act like sleeping pills. Why? Because ADHD is primarily a "running away from boredom." Bored brains feel bad, and physical or mental activity provides that needed stimulation.

The owner of a gently-stimulated ADHD brain doesn't need to keep on doing things or running their brain rapidly in bed to be satisfied (i.e., not bored). Music, white noise, movies, waterbeds, brighter nightlights – all of these can give the same help.

~John I. Bailey Jr., M.D.

John I. Bailey, Jr., MD, Center for Attention & Learning, Mobile, AL
adddoc@bellsouth.net

Why Wait 21 Days?

It's thought that it takes 21 days for something to become a habit.

When you have ADD/ADHD it often takes less than 21 days to become frustrated or bored with a new system or routine. When starting a new system or routine, make sure to evaluate your new system before getting bored or frustrated with it. Pay attention to what is working and what's not working for you.

Begin tweaking your system by adding more of what does work and taking out what doesn't work for you.

The smallest of changes can often make a world of difference.

~Tara McGillicuddy, SCAC

Tara McGillicuddy, SCAC ADD / ADHD Expert
www.youraddcoach.com

You're No Fool

Most people with ADHD are very intelligent. However, we don't always treat ourselves that way. In attempts to meet deadlines, we put an earlier date on our calendar, hoping it will give us the incentive to get it completed. We set clocks and watches a few minutes fast, hoping to get there on time. In reality, I know exactly what the "real" deadline is and just how much time I "really" have before I need to leave the house. I am still not sure why I am trying to fool myself. If these strategies don't work for you either, try honoring your intelligence by entering the actual day and time something is due. Put your clocks hands on the actual time. Quit trying to fool yourself!

~Laurie Dupar, PMHNP, RN, PCC

Laurie Dupar, PMHNP, Certified ADHD Coach, specializes in helping you understand your brain, navigate the treatment maze, reduce your challenges and get things done! www.CoachingforADHD.com

Flip Your Thoughts!

Many of us with ADHD get caught in rumination, or what a former client of mine called "the loopies!"

The best way I've found to break this cycle, once I realize I'm in it, is to flip my thoughts.

How do I do that?

I take a deep breath and then I intentionally think the completely opposite idea!

Often, I write down the new thought in order to anchor the shift. I discovered that by honoring the awareness of my rumination, and using this exercise, I can actually break my chain of repetitive thoughts.

~Dee Doochin, MLAS

Dee Doochin, MLAS, Professional Certified Coach, Certified Mentor Coach, Senior Certified ADHD Coach, wife, mother, grandmother, great-grandmother with ADHD, adventurer, lover of life! www.addupcoach.com

Remember Who You Are

Reconnect to the earth. Plant something. Walk slowly under newly-leafed-out trees. Run your fingers through the grass. Breathe in the sharp winter air. Remember that you are more than you ADHD. You are a magnificent human being who has a right to be here. After all, you won the sperm race! Think about it: of all those other possibilities, YOU were the one who was born. Celebrate your life and give yourself a hug. Or two.

~Linda Roggli, PCC, CLC

Linda Roggli, PCC, CLC Professional Certified Coach, Author of *"Confessions of an ADDiva: midlife in the non-linear lane"*
http://confessionsofanaddiva.net

How to Help Your Non-ADHD Child

The non-ADHD sibling (NAS) often feels as though the ADHD sibling gets more attention, even though some of it may be negative. As a result, other children in your family may feel resentment toward the ADHD sibling, or feel they need to act out or mimic the sibling's behavior in order to get your attention. Therefore, I suggest that you spend as much quality time with your non-ADHD child as possible, and provide them with ample positive reinforcement and attention when possible. The more you know about ADHD, identify how it affects everyone in the family and address those issues, the less conflict there will be.

~Roya Kravetz, ADHD Expert

Roya Kravetz, Life Coach, ADHD Expert and Consultant. Fluent in English, Spanish and Farsi. www.adhdsuccesscoaching.com www.focusforeffectiveness.com

Managing Hyperactivity in the Classroom

ADD/ADHD causes many children to be in constant physical motion. Strategies for combating hyperactivity and increasing focus consist of creative ways to allow children with ADD/ADHD to move in appropriate ways at appropriate times. Releasing energy this way makes it easier for the child to keep their body calmer during work time. Share these with your child's teacher:

- Ask them to run an errand or do a task for you, even if it's just walking across the room to sharpen pencils.
- Have an aid or teacher walk with them around the building for a few minutes when overactive.
- Make sure they never miss recess or P.E. as a punishment; instead have them do work around the classroom.

~Emily Roberts, M.A., LPC

Emily Roberts, M.A., LPC, is a psychotherapist who works with Neurogistics and helps parents balance their child's brain naturally. www.Neurogistics.com

It All Goes Back to Kindergarten

Have you ever visited a Kindergarten class? "Centers" that seem all over the place one minute are corralled the next. Magic wand? No. Each center has a distinct purpose: blocks, reading, cubbies, snack.

Get where I am going? Look at your spaces and have fun designing and labeling (at least mentally) different "centers": sleeping/dressing/audio/reading, etc.

This division works wonders for "keeping track" of our things AND it makes cleaning and organizing easier. It also allows a "chunking down" system to tackle cleaning bigger spaces. Be creative and stretch the Kindegarten centers to your car, garage, locker, and garden!

~Ana Isabel Sánchez

Ana Isabel Sánchez Mom. Wife. Attorney. Certified Coach with ADHD Training. Passion: Helping others take ownership of their lives and focus on their strengths to reach success.

Plan to Glow!

Plan your day on a blank sheet of paper folded in half vertically. Write date at top and list time-specific commitments in order.

Next, add what needs to be accomplished as you think through categories like errands, school, work, etc.

Track your day from this sheet working on to-do's as time allows. Check off as you go.

Capture lists for shopping on the back side. Capture thoughts, ideas or notes on the inside.

Reflect at day's end…and Glow over what you accomplished.

Shift what's left to the next day's plan.

~Robin Nordmeyer, ADHD Coach

Robin Nordmeyer on ADHD www.LifeAheadCoaching.com

Remembering

Use multiple modalities: Incorporate color, seeing, feeling, grasping, speaking, and listening, as you solve challenging situations.

Arrival-Departure: Place important personal items in a special container near entry: wallet/purse, phone, keys, eyeglasses, jewelry and you'll never frantically search for them again.

Errands: On a post-it note, write stops in order. Place on instrument cluster. Check-off as completed. Do it now.

When you remember or see something you've forgotten, telephone, pay, schedule, write, move, or otherwise deal with it immediately if possible. Don't assume you'll remember it later.

Polarity check: Change the negative "shoulds and oughts" to positive. What blocked your success? Improve.

~Glen Hogard, SCAC

Glen Hogard, SCAC, ACO Co-Founder www.GlenHogard.com www.WorldADHD.com www.SynapseCoaching.com http://adhdcoaches.org/circle/first-glen-hogard-award

My "Brains"

One technique I have found extremely useful is to print off a copy of my schedule from Outlook onto an obnoxiously bright colored piece of paper at the beginning of my week. Using this ADD-friendly strategy, I can then place temporary post-it notes on it, write notes on the back, cross off completed tasks, add new ones or shift "to dos" as they arise during the week. The bright color paper makes it easy to find among the other documents on my workspace. At the end of the week I file it in case I need to refer back to it later. As a floor nurse we used a similar system to plan our shift, record important details and called it our "brains".

~Laurie Dupar, PMHNP, RN, PCC

Laurie Dupar, Nurse Practitioner/ ADHD Coach, specializes in helping you understand your brain, navigate the treatment maze, reduce challenges and get things done! www.CoachingforADHD.com Laurie@CoachingforADHD.com

ADHD and Marriage

Every day you create history. Will you create happy, respectful memories? Awareness and clarity in your thoughts and words help you to be heard and understood, to repair misunderstandings, and to meet your needs. Ask yourself: what outcome do I want? How am I asking for what I need? Is this the right time to make a request? Maybe you just need to be heard. If so, say to the other person, "This is a listening moment….!" Aren't we all, after all, just trying to do the best that we can do?

~Dale Davison, M.Sp.Ed.

Dale Davison, M.Sp.Ed., ACAC, Certified ADHD Strategic Life Coach/Marriage, Parents, Students, Professionals
www.dale-davison.com dale@dale-davison.com (847) 269-1055

Top 10 Fidgeting Strategies

Adding stimulation to a primary task makes it easier to remain on task.

A secondary activity (a "fidget"), which is both mindless and makes use of a different sense than that required by the primary one, can be your secret weapon to staying focused.

Here are some of the best strategies:

1. Stand up or pace
2. Walk while conversing
3. Listen to music
4. Chew gum
5. Sit on an exercise ball
6. Race time to finish chores
7. Doodle while taking notes
8. Wiggle your toes
9. Glance out a window
10. Watch a flame or fish tank

~Roland Rotz, Ph.D.

Roland Rotz, Ph.D. and Coach Sarah D. Wright, M.S., A.C.T., internationally-known authors, speakers, and ADHD experts. www.FidgetToFocus.com

Don't Make Lists - Make Outlines

The reason people find lists so daunting is because a list, by definition, implies that there are so many things to do that they must be written down. For some, this is a recipe for disaster. Outlines, however, are much different. First of all, an outline provides the structure that so many of us with ADHD need. Secondly, an outline shows the hierarchy and relationship of its different components and both organizes and breaks down ideas or tasks into increasingly smaller units, which helps fight against the urge to procrastinate because a task seems too large and intimidating. Think of an outline as your roadmap to your goal.

~Robert M. Tudisco, Esq

Robert M. Tudisco, Esq., attorney, writer, ADHD adult and Executive Director of the Edge Foundation, a nonprofit that provides coaching support for students with ADHD. www.edgefoundation.org

Snack for Brain Fuel

For good focus, we should have a complex carbohydrate and a quality protein every 2-3 hours. Snacking healthfully will help to maintain balanced blood glucose levels in the brain. This is important since we need healthy blood glucose levels for energy, brain function and a good sleep cycle. Samples of a good snack might be apple slices dipped in almond or peanut butter or 3 tablespoons of a nut and seed mix with a small amount of dried fruit. Matching a fruit with a protein ensures balanced breakdown of the sugar. A complete protein has the 9 essential amino acids. They are essential because our body cannot make them on their own.

~Pam Machemehl Helmly, CN

Pam Machemehl Helmly, CN, is the Chief Executive Officer for Neurogistics, specializing in Neurotransmitter Testing and Amino Acid Therapy. www.neurogistics.com

Mind Mapping

Do you have a hard time putting your ideas into words that others understand?

One tip: try using mind mapping, using a sequence of post-its, as a way to get your ideas out on a white board, wall, or paper.

If you are a visual person, take a step back to get a new perspective and to help you further clarify your ideas and thoughts so you can write them out for your report or power point slides.

Tip two is to script out the conversations that are hard for you to have, and that cause you to become tongue-tied, or when you just don't want to forget to say something important.

~Deb Bollom, PCC, PC-ACG

Deb Bollom, PCC, PC-ACG, works with entrepreneurs and other adults with ADHD who hate details, feel overwhelmed, and want to discover their strengths and unique ways to move forward. www.d5coaching.com

5 Questions to Ask Your Prescriber

It can be hard to know exactly what to ask your doctor about the ADHD medications you are taking. Following are some suggestions so you feel well-informed:

1. What type of medication is this? How does it help my ADHD?
2. What are common side effects, positive and negative? Are there any that would warrant me to need to call you or stop taking this medication?
3. How will I know if this medication is working? How long does it last?
4. When specifically do I take this medication? With food or without?
5. What is the plan to follow up and monitor this medication's effectiveness?

~Laurie Dupar, PMHNP, RN, PCC

Laurie Dupar, PMHNP, Certified ADHD Coach, specializes in helping you understand your brain, navigate the treatment maze, reduce your challenges and get things done! www.CoachingforADHD.com

Plan is Not a Four-Letter Word

Many people resist planning for a variety of reasons. But "plan" doesn't have to be a four-letter word, as planning allows us to work smarter – not harder. Making a plan is like using a GPS navigation system to help devise the route to get from Point A to Point B. Once you decide your destination or goal, you can plan appropriate steps to get you there, setting intermediate deadlines along the way to pace yourself. It helps to remain flexible, adjusting your plan as necessary. Don't forget to reward yourself for planning the work – and then working the plan!

~Roxanne Fouche, ADHD Coach

Roxanne Fouche, ADHD Coach and Consultant, specializes in working with individuals of all ages with ADHD/LD and related challenges. Roxanne@FocusForEffectiveness.com (858) 484-4749

Develop Your Own Emergency Broadcast System

Everyone has a breaking point. Unfortunately, by the time you reach it, it's too late to stop, and your own momentum pushes you over the edge. People without ADHD seem to have an early warning system alerting them that the cliff is coming; they call it hitting a wall or running out of rope. Many ADHDers don't have this and only realize there was a cliff after they are falling. Don't wait until rock bottom is racing up to meet you. Develop your own alert system. Look for clues from past experiences. Identify the signs. Enlist help in spotting them.

~Rori Boyce, ACC

Rori Boyce, AAC, ADHD Coach Turning Leaf Life Coaching
www.turningleafcoaching.com rori@turningleafcoaching.com
(603) 731-9071

Tips to Manage Time Over Time

- STOP / THINK / THINK THROUGH what you need to do every single day until it becomes a habit.
- NEVER EVER leave home without your calendar/planner. Look at it all day, every day. It will become your best friend!
- Scheduling time and tasks is like a giant puzzle. Every task has a finite amount of time it will take and must have a specific time allocated to completing it.
- Always reschedule in real time. Don't just let things disappear into the black hole of 'later'.
- Don't forget the 25% X factor! Tasks usually take 25% longer than you think they will.

~Nancy Snell, CEC, PCC

Nancy Snell, CEC, PCC, NYC-based professional certified coach/consultant specializing in business/adult ADHD, and information overload solutions. Her bottom line is success with sanity. www.nancysnell.com nancy@nancysnell.com
(212) 517-6488

Make Structure Your Friend

People with ADHD are "allergic" to structure, yet it's the very thing that can help combat ADHD struggles. It creates predictability and minimizes chaos. The top 2 tips my clients find useful are these:

Pre-plan the Day Before

Always plan out the next day before going to bed. This way you'll have in your mind what you are going to do, when, and how. You will wake up more directed and centered.

Create Book Ends

Get up and go to bed at the same time each day. Having regular body rhythms as well as predictability and consistency in your schedule will help increase efficiency.

~Nancy A Ratey, Ed.M., MCC

Nancy A. Ratey, Ed.M., MCC, is a Strategic Life Coach specializing in coaching professionals with ADHD. She is the author of *The Disorganized Mind* www.NancyRatey.com

Get Your Daily/Weekly Tasks Done!

Imagine a piece of paper with a line drawn horizontally across the middle. Above the line you write a maximum of six tasks you have to accomplish that day. Under the line you write the phone calls you have to make for that day. You do this every day except for two days that you leave completely empty. These days are to be used if you have unfinished tasks from the week. It's a wonderful feeling when you cross off a chore one by one. When everything is done, give yourself a nice reward!

~Lilielle Bucks, ADHD Specialist

Lilielle Bucks, ADHD Specialist and ADHD Coach
LilielleBucks@ADHDCoachingSolutions.com

You are the Boss

You own your things and you own your ideas. You are the boss. Therefore, it's up to you whether or not you decide to keep them or do them.

~Carrie Greene, Author

Carrie Greene, speaker, trainer, coach and author of *Chaos to Cash*. She helps entrepreneurs cut through the chaos to make decisions, stop spinning and make more money http://www.CarrieThru.com

"The truly creative individual stands ready to abandon old habits and to acknowledge that life, particularly his own unique life, is rich with possibilities."

~Frank Baron

"Spot" Cleaning

Make a "spot" (circle) out of paper and label it "nothing". You decide how big or small you want these spots. Use your spots, the ones made of paper, to reverse the piles this way:

For a week or two or as long as it takes...

Leave those spots where things tend to accumulate and make sure NOTHING gets put there, EVER!

Now...coffee tables, counter tops, and desks are clutter-free. Isn't that clever?

~Melissa R. Fahrney, M.A., CPC

Melissa Fahrney, M.A., CPC ADHD/Stress Management Coach for kids, college students & adults www.ADDHeartWorks.com www.facebook.com/addheartworks (888) 327-5727 "Don't stress out, master your mountain, with heart!"

Meditation for Focus

I am an ADDer who is highly sensitive to stimulant medication, thus I am not able to take a stimulant to gain the benefits it gives. However, I have found meditation is a great focus tool. It is what I use daily to aid with focus. I spend at least 15 minutes each day, preferably in the morning, sitting in meditation – getting quiet and breathing. Even before I was diagnosed with ADHD, I discovered the days I meditated went much smoother than the ones when I didn't. After my diagnosis, I realized why!

~Dee Doochin, MLAS

Dee Doochin, MLAS, Professional Certified Coach, Certified Mentor Coach, Senior Certified ADHD Coach, wife, mother, grandmother, great-grandmother with ADHD, adventurer, lover of life! www.addupcoach.com

Procrastinator or "Time optimist"?

Most ADHDers racing again to finish late tasks, negatively label themselves a "procrastinator". A more positive/accurate term might be a "time optimist"! Knowing whether you procrastinator (put things off to the last minute) or are a "time optimist" (underestimate the amount of time it takes to get things done) is important. When we procrastinate we are motivated by the urgency of the deadline. The "time optimist" on the other hand misjudges the amount of time needed to accomplish tasks. Go from a "time optimist" to "time realist", by keeping a log of how long it *actually* takes you to complete tasks and then create your "to do" list based on what is humanly possible to accomplish in 24 hours!

~Laurie Dupar, PMHNP, RN, PCC

Laurie Dupar, Certified ADHD Coach, specializes in helping you understand your brain, navigate the treatment maze, reduce your challenges and get things done! www.cCachingforADHD.com Laurie@CoachingforADHD.com

Outsource it!

"Just because you can, doesn't mean you should."

Sure, you can do lots of things. But recognize you can't do it all. Hire out things that you procrastinate or don't enjoy.

~Karen Peak, CPA

Karen Peak - not your typical certified public accountant - runs a successful tax and bookkeeping practice in Northern California, www.karenpeakcpa.com

Landing Pad

The thoughts, concerns, and tasks that float around in one's head take up valuable energy and space, and those with ADHD tendencies have five times the chatter! Create a "Landing Pad" in order to write down those thoughts, offload the "noise," and create space for wise thinking. It must be the same place every time (or one ends up creating more clutter) and something that one really likes to use, look at and feel (or it will not be sustainable). Keep it within reach, and it will create space and peace in your life that might surprise you!

~Ian King, Coach/Speaker

Ian King, Coach/Speaker specializing in ADHD and gifted adults, children, families, and entrepreneurs. Past President of ADHD Coaches Organization & ICF Chicago. www.KingSolutionsInc.com

Sprinting Wins the Day

ADDers are sprinters, not marathon runners. Choose a project or chunk of a project that you'd like to get done quickly. Get ready to work on the project like a sprinter would prepare to run a race. Then, when it's time to work (run your sprint), jump into it and work intensely for the amount of time you allotted. Give it everything you've got! When the bell rings or you cross the finish line, celebrate! Enjoy the satisfaction of realizing progress from your focused effort. Then relax. Good job! Sprints can be really fun and help us accomplish a lot quickly.

~Barbara Luther, MCC

Barbara Luther, Master ADHD Certified Coach, www.WindBeneathYourWings.com President, Professional Association of ADHD Coaches, www.PAACCoaches.org Director of Training, ADD Coach Academy, www.addca.com www.SoaringCoachesCircle.com St. Louis, MO (573) 340-3559

Develop a Team

Develop a support team. Whether you're an adolescent or adult, you need a team to back you up. That team includes family, friends, doctors, coaches, co-workers and whoever else you feel you need and who want you to succeed. With a team behind you, you won't wear out any one person by asking for help all the time. Also, you get the perspective of many different talented people. But remember to give back by offering to help them in your areas of strength so that the relationships are reciprocal. And always say thank you for their support.

~Abigail Wurf, M.Ed.

ADHD Coach Abigail Wurf, M.Ed. My life experience/training make me confident that together, we can make a positive difference in your life! www.abigailwurf.com awurf@verizon.net (202) 244-2234

A Helping Hand

Want to know one of the biggest secrets to success? You can't do it all. That's why most successful business people are great at delegating tasks to others. Don't waste your time and energy doing things you hate. Enlist help from others, or offer to exchange tasks you dislike for ones you enjoy. Business people with ADHD often struggle with organizational issues, such as paperwork or scheduling, so ask or hire someone to do it for you. This way, you will still be able to do what you love, enjoy what you do best and live life to the fullest.

~Dr. Billi, Ph.D.

The AttentionB Method, Neuro-Cognitive Behavioral Therapy/Coaching with Dr. Billi, Ph.D. Express your Unique Voice using my Unique Expressive Art Therapy Techniques. www.AttentionB.com DrBilli@AttentionB.com (855) Dr Billi

Best Jobs for ADHD

I am frequently asked, "What is the best job for someone with ADHD?" The best career match for someone with ADHD is one that they are interested in, that they are passionate about, that highlights their gifts and talents and provides them the opportunity to minimize their challenges. People with ADHD can be anything they want, including: doctors, lawyers, teachers, athletes, actors, police, firefighters, accountants, writers, genetic counselors, environmentalists, therapists, entrepreneurs, engineers, public speakers, artists, musicians...the list is endless because the best career for someone with ADHD is a career that is uniquely suited to them. What do you *really* want to do?

~Laurie Dupar, PMHNP, RN, PCC

Laurie Dupar, Certified ADHD Coach, specializes in helping you understand your brain, navigate the treatment maze, reduce your challenges and get things done! www.CoachingfofADHD.com Laurie@CoachingforADHD.com

Easy Note-Taking for Office or Classroom

Here's a tip for remembering verbal instructions or written information: Ask instructors if you can videotape them using your cell phone or take a picture of the written instructions. Most people carry cell phones that do everything. Cells were allowed at my school, so after I wrote instructions for a test or class assignment on the board, I allowed students to take a picture of the information. For students not allowed to use phones, parents can ask the teacher to take a picture using their own cell phone or videotape the spoken instructions and upload it to their website.

~Sandy Alletto Corbin, M.A., SCAC

Ms. Sandy Alletto Corbin, M.A., SCAC, Certified Senior ADHD Coach and Advocate working with families, teens and women. She can be reached at http://www.lifecoachsandyalletto.com

Misunderstood!

I just say what's on my mind and trouble begins!

The struggle to control blurting out can be difficult. Why? If we don't say something as soon as we think of it, we know we'll forget what we wanted to say!

But too often the comment we blurt out is too harsh or not well thought out. Then we have to defend our statement and ourselves.

Rehearse these two simple statements until they become the filter between what you want to say and if you should say it:

1. What's the purpose?
2. What can I expect?

This will minimize embarrassing moments. It's like mom said: "Think before you speak!"

~Joyce A. Kubik

Joyce Kubik, ADHD Coach www.bridgetosuccess.net

Forgive Yourself. Every Day.

One of the common experiences of having ADHD is feeling ashamed. This shamefulness can come from feeling like you can't ever live up to your potential, being habitually late, experiencing impulsive desires, or the inability to listen or focus on conversations. Whatever the source of shame, it is likely magnified by feeling like you've disappointed a loved one, starting with yourself.

It's important to forgive yourself for the past...every day! This can be tough, however, knowing that many struggles and challenges are attributable to having ADHD, and not due to my lack of effort or good intentions, has allowed me to replace that shamefulness with a pure sense of freedom.

~David Sloan

David Sloan, 31 yrs old, recently diagnosed with ADD Columbia, SC

Grammie Knows Best

As a grandmother of children with ADHD, I found that providing structure, consistency and predictability in my home when my grandchildren visited was important to everyone's enjoyment. Try these tips:

- Have a table and chairs just their size. Play dough, coloring, crafts, and rolling cinnamon rolls were favorites at the "kids'" table.
- An old-fashioned doll house, legos and basket of books are great for quiet, low-stimulation play options.
- Outside, a sturdy, simple swing set, basket of balls, bug-catching nets and water play allowed for stretching "big muscles" and exploring when the walls felt like they were closing in.

~Joanne Melton, Grandmother

Joanne Melton, grandmother of 10 "extremely special grandchildren" (three with ADHD).

Listen Up! 5 Tips for Auditory Learners

As an auditory leaner, you learn best when you hear information. Follow these tips to help you make the most of your learning style:

Tip # 1: Recite information you want to remember several times. Read text out loud. This helps to retain information.

Tip # 2: Participate in group and class discussions.

Tip # 3: Use flash cards. Read cards out loud when reviewing.

Tip # 4: Present information to others orally. If you can teach it, you know it.

Tip # 5: Have white noise or consistent music playing in the background when studying. The music should not distract you from the task at hand.

~Laurie Moore Skillings, SCAC

Laurie Moore Skillings, Senior Certified ADHD Coach, specializes in working with teens that have a hard time with school. Laurie can be reached at laurie@addwithease.com

Use Triggers & Forget About Remembering

Remember things easier when you assoicate them with PHYSICAL TRIGGERS.

- When you step out of the kitchen, consider the transition a trigger to 'look back' to see what you've left out on the counter, or if the cabinet doors and drawers are open.
- When you touch the doorknob to leave home, let it trigger a 'look for' your keys, wallet, purse, bookbag or whatever you should be taking out the door.
- If you need to buy something, write it on paper you have to step on to get out of the house, then 'look down' and take it with you.

~Susan Karyn Lasky, MA, SCAC

Susan Lasky is a Master ADHD Strategist, Productivity & Organization Coach, helping adults and older students to get things done and enjoy life! Susan@SusanLasky.com (914) 373-4787

The Caffeine Myth

Caffeine is often used to help with focus. The problem with using any kind of stimulant is that when the dopamine gets pushed out into the synapse, serotonin is lost in an effort to "reign" in the excess dopamine. Dopamine is an excitatory or stimulating neurotransmitter, and serotonin is our main inhibitory or calming neurotransmitter. The brain constantly tries to balance between the two. Individuals using caffeine often have to use more and more over time to get the same benefit. Unfortunately, they just deplete their serotonin more and more when this occurs.

~Pam Machemehl Helmly, CN

Pam Machemehl Helmly, CN, is the Chief Executive Officer for Neurogistics, specializing in Neurotransmitter Testing and Amino Acid Therapy. www.neurogistics.com

Handle Impulse Spending

Do you spend impulsively when you are out and about? Try leaving the plastic money at home and just taking along cash. Using cash creates an automatic limit on what you can spend. Plus, it makes money tangible and real. It's easier to experience the money going out when you can see and feel it leave your wallet. Try it!

~Sarah D. Wright, M.S., A.C.T.

Sarah D. Wright, M.S., A.C.T., internationally-known ADHD coach, speaker, author, expert, and founding Board Member of the ADHD Coaches Organization. Contact her at Sarah@FocusForEffectiveness.com

To-Do Lists

There are many tools and suggestions on how to keep track of your "To-Do" list. Problem is that if it doesn't work for you, what good is it? Try different tools and techniques until you find what works for you, no matter how simple or low-tech it might be. I keep two lists: one for items that need to be done that day and another for those that have multiple steps and will take several days/weeks to complete. I write the daily list in my basic spiral notebook. For the other, longer tasks, I use an excel spreadsheet.

~Anonymous

There is H.O.P.E

Don't silently struggle with the challenges of ADHD, feeling overwhelmed, frazzled, discouraged or disorganized. Instead, know that help is available, knowledge is power and you can find fulfillment, focus and the positive energy to reach your dreams. Finding help to succeed --- in any way --- provides the foundation for a more positive attitude that ADHD is less about deficits and disabilities and more about different abilities, creativity and understanding. Get help to learn about that unique and amazing ADHD mind, optimize your potential for excellence .....and soar! Let the journey begin!

~Beverly Rohman, SCAC

Beverly Rohman is founder of The Learning Connections, LLC, and Senior Certified ADHD Coach/Learning Consultant working with families, adults, college students, and professionals. Easton, MD www.thelearningconnections.net

Be Honest with Yourself

Be honest with yourself. If you find that you're consistently running late, it doesn't mean you should work faster, or that others can do something faster. It simply means that you need to add more time to how long you give yourself.

~Carrie Greene, Speaker

Carrie Greene, speaker, trainer, coach and author of *Chaos to Cash*. She helps entrepreneurs cut through the chaos to make decisions, stop spinning and make more money. http://www.CarrieThru.com

What is Procrastination?

By definition, procrastination is: "To put off intentionally doing something that should be done." When your ADD makes you stuck and unable to take action, are you really procrastinating? Most of the time, we ADDers have the best of intentions; we don't want to disappoint ourselves, our bosses, or our partners by not following through with our commitments--again. Because there are strong negative connotations and an undertone of moral judgment to the word procrastination, it can be helpful to reframe this state as simply being "stuck" or overwhelmed. The words you choose to describe your own challenges matter!

~Lynne A. Edris, ACG

Lynne is a woman with ADD, Mom to an ADHD Teen, a professional ADD Coach, and CHADD Parent 2 Parent Trainer. All ADD, All the Time!

Write Stuff Down!

If you have a problem remembering where you put your keys, how can you depend on that same brain to remember the details of a report due next week?

In all things, think about the next step in that big project. Make the next step so small you can do it before you can think, "Na, I don't feel like doing that."

Write that down.

"Make a doctor's appointment" is not the next thing. Find his phone number and write it down is.

"Paint the basement floor" is not the next thing. Get all that crap out of the basement might be!

~Kerch McConlogue, PCC, CPCC

Kerch McConlogue, PCC, CPCC www.mapthefuture.com
(410) 929-3274

Stop Ruminating!

Ruminating is the habit of turning things over in your mind again and again and again and it's often hard to stop once you get started. You can waste a lot of mental and emotional energy down this black hole. Worrying can be a habit, and habits can be broken.

1. Notice when you are ruminating; acknowledge it, and tell yourself to stop. NOW!
2. Immediately do something else! Sing, walk, jump up and down, text a friend...anything but ruminate.
3. Change your focus...look at something else...it will bring you back to the real world.
4. Set aside a day and time limit each week to ruminate. Worry all you want during that time and then...move on.
5. Schedule time to think about what you are grateful for. You've allowed time for the rumination…find time for happiness!

~Laurie Dupar, PMHNP, RN, PCC

Laurie Dupar, Nurse Practitioner, ADHD Coach, specializes in helping you understand your brain, navigate the treatment maze, reduce your challenges and get things done! www.CoachingforADHD.com

Job Success: Survival Tips from an ADD Pro That Survived!

- Identify and write down what you need to maximize your effectiveness so that you can articulate it to your boss and develop strategies together.
- Don't be afraid to ask for small accommodations.
- Advocate for yourself. If you are flooded with too much information, ask your manager to please repeat what he/she said.
- Follow through: If you say you are going to do something, DO IT or let your boss know why.
- Write down everything 24/7. NEVER rely on memory!
- Clarify, clarify, clarify when you feel confused at all. Take the risk even if you think you "already asked once."

~Nancy Snell, CEC, PCC

Nancy Snell, CEC, PCC, NYC-professional certified coach/consultant specializing in business/adult ADHD, and information overload solutions. Her bottom line is success with sanity. www.nancysnell.com nancy@nancysnell.com (212) 517-6488

Special Time With Your Child:

- Spend time one-on-one with your child on a regular basis.
- Let your child choose the activity. If he/she just wants to watch TV with you, that is fine.
- When playing with your child, let him/her direct the play. This allows your child the opportunity to lead, without fear of judgment or punishment!
- Making it brief is always better than not making any time at all.
- Make sure you are relaxed and ready to follow your child's lead.
- Let your child know that you are enjoying his/her company.

~Roya Kravetz, Life Coach

Roya Kravetz, Credentialed Life Coach, ADHD Coach and Consultant, and Parent Educator. Specializes in ADHD Coaching and/or related Challenges. www.adhdsuccesscoaching.com

"We must be willing to get rid of the life we've planned, so as to have the life that is waiting for us. The old skin has to be shed before the new one can come."

~Joseph Campbell

Keep Intentions Front and Center

We have really good intentions each day to eat healthily, keep our spending in check, and move our goals along. Yet the intensity and variety of life can make these intentions difficult to follow throughout an entire day. Science has solidly proven that recording our intentions and behaviors throughout the day helps us stay present and attentive to our goals, yet most of us resist this simple practice, telling ourselves it's too hard or preferring not to know. A colorful composition journal offers space to record your day's notes, calls, things you want to remember and get done, what you eat, what you spend, and how you feel. One easy place, a good record. Easy peazy!

~Barbara Luther, MCC

Barbara Luther, Master ADHD Certified Coach, www.WindBeneathYourWings.com President, Professional Association of ADHD Coaches, www.PAACCoaches.org Director of Training, ADD Coach Academy, www.addca.com www.SoaringCoachesCircle.com St. Louis, MO (573) 340-3559

Too Perfect for Your Own Good?

Try a growth mindset. Our abilities are not fixed. We get better at things we practice. We learn from our efforts. Social psychologists tell us that a fixed mindset is simply incorrect.

All those efforts with mediocre or worse results are learning experiences that lead us to success, as long as we adopt a growth mindset.

Another way of saying this is choose a Getting-Better, as opposed to the Be-Good, mindset. You will cope with challenges more easily, and continue moving toward your goal.

~Kathy Peterson, ADHD Coach

Kathy Peterson, ADHD Coach since 1994, works with adults, primarily professionals, entrepreneurs, and people in corporate business and science; located in Arlington, MA; credentialed by ICF. www.petersoncoaching.com

Get an Accurate Time Sense

Guess how many minutes an activity will take you and write it down. Then, write how many minutes it REALLY took. Compare the two and determine how "off" you were. (Example: if you guessed 20 minutes and it really took 60 minutes, it took 3 times as long as you thought.) Do this for many random activities, note your patterns and adjust your time predictions accordingly; if you take 3 times as long for many things, multiply your predictions by three. This will dramatically improve your ability to plan and be on time!

~Bonnie Mincu, SCAC

Bonnie Mincu, Senior ADHD Coach and founder of "THRIVE with ADD," has numerous classes, tools and resources on Adult ADHD challenges at www.thrivewithadd.com bonnie@bonniemincu.com (914) 478-0071

Frazzled and Forgot What Works?

Create your own "ADHD Tool Box." Get a shoebox or plastic box (this is your "tool box"). Decorate it with beads, markers, macaroni, feathers, sequins, pictures, stickers, anything that brings you joy.

Next, add your "ADHD Tools." These include anything that helps you "remember" how to manage and/or take charge of your ADHD. "Tools" are items that trigger your memory for what worked in the past or inspire ideas for new solutions to try. Such items as a special quote, a note saying "BREATHE," a picture of an oxygen-mask (take care of yourself first), sea shells, fabric, photos, stones, or whatever object is a positive memory of success.

~Cindy Giardina, Certified Coach

Cindy Giardina, Professional Certified Coach through ICF, Specializing in ADHD. NJ/USA Contact Coach Cindy and share what's in YOUR tool box! www.kaleidoscope-coaching.com
cindy@kaleidoscope-coaching.com (973) 694-5077

Take Two

Duplication is surely the road to ADHD happiness. Collect duplicate sets of makeup (one for car, purse, home, office); lots of inexpensive reader glasses can live all over the house; duplicate bottles of medication help you remember to take those pesky pills; multiple sets of measuring cups and measuring spoons in the kitchen speed your cooking; plant a pair of working scissors at every desk, in the kitchen, bedroom and bathroom; buy an extra lens cover for your camera just in case (they're cheap). Save yourself a world of embarrassment and frustration–try duplication!

~Linda Roggli, PCC/CLC

Linda Roggli, PCC/CLC Professional Certified Coach, Author of *"Confessions of an ADDiva: midlife in the non-linear lane"* http://confessionsofanaddiva.net

Manage Perfectionism with the TQC Triangle

In any project, there are three criteria to consider: the amount of time it will take, the quality of the end result, and the cost. We typically give up one of these three to get the other two. For example, if I want high quality fast, then it will cost a lot. If I don't care how long something takes, I can get good quality at a good price. Perfectionists want all three, which means they usually give away lots of their time and end up being underpaid for the quality of their work. Before you impulsively lock onto the "only" way to do something, check to see which two criteria are most important. That may save you lots of unappreciated effort and frustration.

~Barbara Luther, MCC

Barbara Luther, Master ADHD Certified Coach, www.WindBeneathYourWings.com President, Professional Association of ADHD Coaches, www.PAACCoaches.org Director of Training, ADD Coach Academy, www.addca.com www.SoaringCoachesCircle.com St. Louis, MO (573) 340-3559

Managing Interruptions

"Why do I answer the phone when she calls?"

"She keeps me on for 45 minutes every time."

"What an idiot!"

The voice in my head was talking about me again.

Interruptions are hard to resist if you have ADHD. The trick is to set limits. Let voicemail take the call and reply via email. Or, write "scripts" to post near your phone: "I'm in the middle of something." "I have something in 5 minutes." "When can I get back to you?" Teach others that your time is YOURS. They will think twice before expecting to waste your time again.

~Casey Dixon, MSEd., CTACC

Casey Dixon, MSEd., CTACC www.dixonlifecoaching.com

Around the World with ADHD

ADHD affects approximately 3-5% of the world's population. Most likely, there are many more people with ADHD than have been diagnosed. ADHD is not gender specific and is ethnically diverse. Male or female, in the United States or South Africa or Iceland, people with ADHD share challenges of either inattention, hyperactivity, impulsivity or a combination of the three. Know that you are not alone. Know that you share a unique brain style with millions of people around the world. People with ADHD are an amazing group of creative, resourceful, adventurous individuals. Reach out. Learn more about ADHD. Welcome to our world!

~Laurie Dupar, PMHNP, RN, PCC

Laurie Dupar, PMHNP, Certified ADHD Coach, specializes in helping you understand your brain, navigate the treatment maze, reduce challenges and get things done! Laurie@CoachingforADHD.com (916) 791-1799

The Best Decision Right Now?

Create positive momentum one good decision at a time with this daily mantra. How can something this simple help? We actually listen to what we say to ourselves. Many ADHDers become overwhelmed by long "to-do" lists or complex projects. While it may feel easier in the moment to put things off and promise to do them later, you are actually tripling your stress. If instead you ask, "What is the best decision I can make right now?" you will force yourself into present thinking. Most often, your best decision will be the one that meets your goals.

~Linda Richmand, Life Coach

Linda Richmand, Business, Career, and Life Coach specializing in adult AD/H/D. www.CoachRichmand.com (914) 330-9103

Respect Your Needs

Many times we say yes to everything else but deny ourselves the things we personally need. Don't sell yourself short by saying yes to everyone but yourself. Know your needs and don't give up on them. For example, I have a specific routine I must follow each morning. I must wake up with music, hear my grandchildren's voices and take a warm bath for 30 minutes. It's the transition I need from sleep to facing the world. If I don't follow this routine, my day feels crazy. Like oxygen masks on airplanes are essential for safety purposes, it's necessary to take care of yourself before you can take care of others.

~Dr. Billi, Ph.D.

The AttentionB Method, Neuro-Cognitive Behavioral Therapy/Coaching www.AttentionB.com (855) Dr Billi

Compensation Strategies for Adults

Adults don't necessarily outgrow ADHD, they just learn to compensate for it. Dr. Robert Wells, Ph.D., Director of Pediatric Research at Valley Children's Hospital in Fresno, Ca, discovered that successful men and women with ADHD:

- Set up rituals to get through repetitive tasks.
- Use lists to retain large amounts of information.
- Write down their thoughts to control impulsive behaviors.
- Work in jobs with a variety of different tasks each day.
- Are in charge of themselves and their time but use structure to get tasks complete.
- Delegate.

~Anonymous

Play Big

"*Life is too short to be small.*" ~ Benjamin Disraeli, former British Prime Minister

What I want for you is for you to play "big" in the areas of life that you want to play "big." That may be in having a great relationship with your significant other, being the best parent you can, advancing in your company, having optimal health and wellness, growing your company as CEO. Whatever it is, it requires that you decide where you want to go and what you want to be, do, and have.

~Robb Garrett, MA, MCC, ACT

Robb Garrett, MA, MCC, ACT, President of ADHD Coaches Organization www.adhdcoaches.org

Slow Down to Go Fast

One erroneous thought process of those who have ADHD tendencies is the internal belief that if one is under pressure, one must go faster in order to succeed. Unfortunately, this creates a great deal of stress and causes the body to release chemicals that shut down the area of the brain that supports wise decision making. So, the next time you notice the urgency is rising, physically slow down. Breathe, and take time to process your next best steps. You will then have allowed the chemical rush to subside and will create much more effective and sustainable action.

~Ian King, Coach/Speaker

Ian King, Coach/Speaker specializing in ADHD and gifted adults, children, families, and entrepreneurs. Past President of ADHD Coaches Organization & ICF Chicago.www.KingSolutionsInc.com

Boost Your Achilles' Heel for Procrastination and Deadlines at Work

- Break it down with the steps and resources needed for completion.
- Designate a folder, bin, or station to collect what's needed ahead of time.
- Create urgency by making the task the first thing you do before distractions set in.
- Buddy up by finding a partner to work side by side with or mirror your timing with others doing the same thing in the office.
- Build accountability and arrange with a spouse, co-worker, friend, or coach to text a follow-up note when accomplished.

~Robin Nordmeyer, ADHD Coach

Robin Nordmeyer, ADHD Coach www.LifeAheadCoaching

Awareness

Awareness is the first step to change. Until I become aware of and totally accept a situation, there is no way I can hope to change it. I have to own something before I can change it. Otherwise, I will find a million excuses or reasons why it is the way it is and keep on doing things the same way. Once I become aware of it, own it, and own the desire to change it, change can happen. It doesn't matter whether it is a habit or a belief. Awareness, ownership and desire are the elements of change.

~Dee Doochin, MLAS

Dee Doochin, MLAS, Professional Certified Coach, Certified Mentor Coach, Senior Certified ADHD Coach, wife, mother, grandmother, great-grandmother with ADHD, adventurer, lover of life! www.addupcoach.com

Focus on Your "End Game"

You can shine in interviews and important meetings when you focus on your "end game."

What information do you want your listener to walk away knowing about you, your idea or product? Start by making a comprehensive list. Don't simply write, "I am a self-starter." Substantiate each statement with examples or stories. Keep going until you cannot think of any more to say. As you read the list, your confidence will grow. It is particularly empowering to practice saying these true things aloud to someone you trust. Voila! No more worries; you are prepared to knock the socks off of anyone!

~Linda Richmond, Life Coach

Linda Richmond, Business, Career, and Life Coach specializing in adult AD/H/D www.CoachRichmond.Com (914) 330-9103

Would You Please Stop Talking!

You're sitting in your office cubicle and the person's voice a few cubicles away is just driving you crazy. It's all you can hear, and you have a major deadline to meet in just three hours. You could ask the person to talk quieter, but it may not be appropriate. Instead, look for a quiet room, such as a conference room, that will allow you to focus and complete your project. Likewise, if you work out of your home and your surroundings are not allowing you to focus, take your work elsewhere, such as a quiet room in a community library.

~Joyce Kubik, ADHD Coach

Joyce Kubik, Author, Presenter, Researcher, and ADHD Coach & Skills Trainer, coaches adults, college students and is a coach trainer. Avon Lake, Ohio

Listening ....Whadya Say?

When was the last time you listened to someone? When was the last time someone listened to you? Being listened to is one of the most powerful experiences you can have. Listening with intent is an art that needs to be practiced by all of us. Next time your teen/spouse/partner/child asks you a question, stop, look and focus on just that person. If the doorbell /phone rings, don't answer it. Allow yourself to be fully present for the other person and see how listening can empower others and improve relationships.

~Hazel Brief, PCC

Hazel K. Brief, MSW, PCC, www.SyngergetiCoaching.Com

Three Top ADHD Medication Pitfalls

As a trained Psychiatric Mental Health Nurse Practitioner, my experience has me uniquely tuned into the effectiveness of medication management of ADHD. Typically, there are three areas that keep someone from experiencing full effectiveness of their ADHD medications: wrong medication, wrong dose or wrong time. If you don't think your medication is working for you, explore changes in these three areas with your prescriber. Ask about alternative medications, consider changing the dose or adjusting when you take the medication to allow for the onset of its action and when it is wearing off.

~Laurie Dupar, PMHNP, RN, PCC

Laurie Dupar, PMHNP, Certified ADHD Coach, specializes in helping you understand your brain, navigate the treatment maze, reduce your challenges and get things done! www.CoachingforADHD.com

The Dreaded "To-Do" List

One major thing I have found with all of my friends or clients that have ADHD is that a list of things to do is so overwhelming, they don't know where to begin so it just does not even get started.

People may say, "What's the problem? Just start at the top and work your way down the list." Not that simple. What works best is to only put one or two things on your list and finish them, then add another. This is very important for spouses, family members or co-workers to note for the ADDer. Work gets done……. less stress!

~Joey Bishop, ADHD Coach

Joey Bishop, ADD/ADHD Life Coach www.ADDvanceforward.com

Find Your Voice

"I haven't lost it," she said.

Do you speak up for yourself? For what you want, what you need?

"But they already know, and I really don't like fights."

How many times a day do we skip an opportunity to find our voice AND, most important, to share it? Yelling has nothing to do with it. It is all about self-respect and acknowledgement.

Let's try. What do you want to say? Really. Don't go to your brain; it all lies in your body. Feel it and let it flow out with the sound of your voice.

~Ana Sánchez, ADHD Coach

Ana Sánchez, sassy,authentic & witty mom, wife, Certified ADHD Life Coach, friend, lawyer, passionate explorer of strengths. Curious about possibilities from 'I'm Able' stance.

A Roadmap for Teens

Not sure where to start or where you're supposed to end pp? Do you find it difficult to manage a long-term project, write an essay, be prepared for upcoming events, or know what needs to be done first – or next – in a task? Figure out what works best for you by creating a roadmap and then strengthening your executive functions skills of planning/prioritization.

How to create a personal ROADMAP

1. Review task(s) to be done
2. Order the steps that need to be done
3. Ask if the steps make sense
4. Determine sub-steps if needed
5. Make checklists
6. Apply tools
7. Provide accommodations

~Laurie Moore Skillings, SCAC

Laurie Moore Skillings, SCAC is an ADHD Teen Coach. She helps teens understand ADHD and how it can affect their lives.

"Success is going from failure to failure without losing your enthusiasm."

~Abraham Lincoln

External Accountability

External sources of accountability can help us stay on track. This doesn't have to cost a lot.

Here are a few examples:

- You can hire a high school student for minimum wage to assist you. The student gains valuable skills while you delegate filing, data entry, errand running, etc. You gain the extra motivation to perhaps finish that task that is waiting. They can also sit next to you while you noodle through a task.
- Set reminders on your smart phone or electronic calendar.
- You can also work with a fabulous coach who targets specific matters.

~Karen Peak, CPA

Karen Peak - not your typical certified public accountant - runs a successful tax and bookkeeping practice in Northern California, helping entrepreneurial clients from coast to coast.
www.karenpeakcpa.com

A Cluttered Space is a Cluttered Mind

You didn't see it coming. You're busy, you're curious, and you're interested in so many things!

Projects, papers, and to-do's accumulate. Piles begin to appear and stuff is everywhere. Suddenly you feel cluttered, stressed, and overwhelmed.

Relieve your mind by clearing your space. Start with these simple ideas:

- Before you begin, make a plan.
- Be willing to say "No!" and let go.
- Honor and display what you keep, so you keep less.
- Put everything in its own place.
- If you're stuck, get help from a professional organizer.
- If you're still overwhelmed, a therapist can help

~Roland Rotz, PhD

Roland Rotz, Ph.D., internationally-known author, speaker, and ADHD expert. www.DocRotz.com

Reduce Friction to Increase Task Completions

Completing non-interesting and non-stimulating things is often difficult for people with ADHD. To increase your completion ratio, reduce friction. Friction is anything that makes something harder to do. Reduce friction = reduce barriers to task completion. Think of what you could do to make a task easier; take less time, less effort, less money, fewer steps, become quicker or more convenient. For example, if you need to oil your bike chain, have the oil & rag near the bike in a visible spot. Easier to do = more likely you'll do it. More steps, harder, more out of the way, more effort = less likely to get done.

~Pete Quily

Pete Quily, Adult ADHD Coach www.ADDCoach4u.com

When the Dresser is the Floor

The plan: I went to a container store and bought 6 large wire baskets, the kind that normally slide into a metal frame. But I didn't buy the frame. Then I got a book shelf where the shelves adjusted and created large spaces between shelves. I sorted the clothes inside the baskets, then placed them on the shelves. This was doable! The clothes were visible from most angles so the search and throw on the floor method was out. It was also easy to toss them back in if they weren't chosen for the day's look.

~Sandy Alletto Corbin, M.A., SCAC

Ms. Sandy Alletto Corbin, Certified Senior ADHD Coach and Advocate working with families, teens and women. She can be reached at http://www.lifecoachsandyalletto.com

Take a Seat

Minimizing distraction and increasing the ability for students to attend is key to their success in a classroom. One common strategy is to have a student sit in the front row, close to the teacher where they can be kept on task. Unfortunately, this is not always the best seat in the house for every student. Trips by classmates to the teacher's desk, opening and closing of the door, or even the hum of the overhead projector may be even more distracting. When choosing the best seat for your child/student, look at all the options, taking into consideration traffic patterns, classroom noises and other students.

~Laurie Dupar, PMHNP, RN, PCC

Laurie Dupar, PMHNP, Certified ADHD Coach, specializes in helping you understand your brain, navigate the treatment maze, reduce your challenges and get things done! www.CoachingforADHD.com

What Was I Supposed to Do?

It's important to be competent at work, but most adults with ADHD have working memory deficits. This makes it difficult to remember a long list of things to do! Here are some strategies that work for me:

1. Keep a notebook or calendar of things to do as soon as they are assigned.
2. Write a reminder on the calendar to begin work now on a project due next week!
3. Don't take assignments in the hallway; tell colleagues to put all inquiries in your mailbox or on your desk.
4. Keep a copy of all projects.
5. Get a signature or date stamp when projects are turned in!
6. Keep files and folders organized for easy use.
7. Keep detailed notes of casual meetings, staff development meetings and departmental meetings.

~Lisa-Anne Ray-Byers

Lisa-Anne Ray-Byers, Speech-Language Pathologist, Columnist and Author www.AskLisaAnne.com

Before School Morning Tips

Many families find school mornings stressful. The following tips might help:

- Develop the habit of putting completed homework in a specific place in the child's binder and placing the backpack and other needed items by the door.
- Lay out the next day's clothes the night before to decrease the number of decisions needed in the morning.
- Make lunches in the evening and refrigerate them, as necessary.
- Post a checklist of the morning routine with as much detail as your child needs (e.g., brush teeth, comb hair, take medication, etc.) and have him check items off as they are completed.

~Roxanne Fouche, ADHD Coach

Roxanne Fouche, ADHD Coach and Consultant, specializes in working with individuals of all ages with ADHD/LD and related challenges. Roxanne@FocusForEffectiveness.com (858) 484-4749

A Simple Organizing Trick for Work or Home

Here's a simple organizing trick to use at work or at home when you're facing an overwhelming pile of clutter on your desk or table and you don't know where to start.

1. Drape a sheet or blanket over all but a small chunk of the clutter.
2. Put away, throw away and organize the bit of clutter that shows.
3. Once you've cleared the first bit, slide the sheet over to expose another chunk of the clutter, tackling it as you did in Step 2 above.
4. Keep moving the sheet until the clutter is all gone.

~Dana Rayburn, SCAC

Dana Rayburn, Senior Certified ADHD Coach, helps business owners, professionals and ADHD adults get organized and outsmart their Attention Deficit to live successful and satisfying lives. www.danarayburn.com

How to Sit When You Can't Sit Still

Meditation is a powerful tool for managing ADHD. This can feel like another cruel jab, as meditating properly requires everything ADHD makes impossible. We picture Zen masters wrapped in stillness, surrounded by silence, relishing the calm serenity provided by a quiet mind. But you can make meditation work for you. Let go of the idea that there is a proper way to meditate. Invite your brain to participate. Engage your senses. Use a mantra. Light incense. Use prayer beads. Give yourself permission to move. Instead of fighting against yourself on the road to inner peace, make your own path.

~Rori Boyce, ACC

Rori Boyce, ACC, ADHD Coach Turning Leaf Life Coaching
www.turningleafcoaching.com rori@turningleafcoaching.com
(603) 731-9071

What if All Institutions Copied the Google Model?

At Google, the employees allot 20 percent of their work time to brainstorming novel ideas. In 2005, 50 percent of the new products launched by Google were conceived during this brief period of time.

People with ADHD are known to be very creative and "out-of-the-box" thinkers…perfect brainstormers!

What if all institutions/companies/schools followed the Google example and gave more importance to creativity, imagination and forward thinking? My guess is that everybody would benefit. It is time we put less emphasis on linear thinking and value more creativity in order to achieve a balance…just imagine!

~Roya Kravetz, ADHD Coach

Roya Kravetz, ADHD Coach and Consultant. Working with individuals, families and small businesses. Fluent in English, Spanish and Farsi. roya@adhdsuccesscoaching.com

Saying "No" for the Positive

ADHD can cause financial impulsivity that can lead to wasted money and increased stress. Learn to say "no" to gain positive control over your financials. Follow these skill-building steps:

- Identify situations where you make impulsive purchases.
- Rehearse saying "no" before entering the situation. For example, saying, "No thanks, I'm just looking," before going shopping at a store with persuasive salespeople.
- Practice your statement five times before getting to the store.
- Evaluate your progress when leaving the store and praise yourself to celebrate success.

It takes daily practice to build this skill. Start practicing today to turn "no" into a positive!

~Laura Rolands, ADHD Coach

Laura Rolands is the founder of www.MyAttentioncoach.com, where she regularly helps clients with ADHD / ADD say "no" to the impulsive choices in their life.

How to Overcome the Clutter

Look at your space as though you were seeing it for the first time. Sometimes we become blind to the reality of our environment because of habit, familiarity or avoidance. Decide that you will only keep items that you love, need or that hold good memories. If you aren't sure, pack it away for six months, then decide. Otherwise, bless someone else with the stuff you no longer need. When putting things away, group like with like so that similar items are kept together in an appropriate "home." Clearly label the "home" so no one in the house forgets what goes where.

~Susan Lasky, ADHD Strategist

Susan Lasky is a Master ADHD Strategist and Productivity & Organization Coach, helping adults and older students to get things done and enjoy life! www.SusanLasky.com
Susan@SusanLasky.com (914) 373-4787

Myths About Stimulants

Stimulant medications have been used in the treatment of ADHD for over 50 years, yet fear leading to limiting choices, still exists. Knowledge equals power, so following are commonly held myths and accompanying facts to clarify:

- Myth: Stimulants are addictive. Fact: No evidence exists that stimulant medication taken as prescribed leads to addiction. In fact, most people forget to take it at all!
- Myth: Taking stimulant medications leads to drug abuse. Fact: Research has shown that treating ADHD appropriately with medication *decreases* the risk of drug abuse.
- Myth: Stimulant medications will make my child shorter. Fact: Studies have shown that height differences in children with ADHD were not related to use of ADHD medication.

Choose based on fact, not fear.

~Laurie Dupar, PMHNP, RN, PCC

Laurie Dupar, Nurse Practitioner & ADHD Coach Laurie@CoachingforADHD.com

Change Your Attitude, Not Yourself

Don't change who you are just because you have ADHD. Instead, change your attitude. Be positive. Relate to yourself as a winner. Figure out your priorities. What's holding you back from living the life you want? If there's a particular habit that's making you suffer, recognize it. The AttentionB Method trains you how to modify your bad habits into a strategy that works for you, not against you. Practice and revise new strategies until you find what works best and you're happy with the results. Like champions, you will succeed if you're willing to get out of your comfort zone, but still be yourself.

~Dr. Billi, PhD.

The AttentionB Method, Neuro-Cognitive Behavioral Therapy/Coaching with Dr. Billi, Ph.D. Live a Happier and Fuller Life. Perform at Your Peak Potential. www.AttentionB.com DrBilli@AttentionB.com (855) Dr Billi

Just Say "No!"

I always say that physical clutter begets mental clutter. But the clutter in our lives is often more than the "stuff" around us. It can also be the "stuff" in our schedule and our obligations. The ability to say "No" to time and schedule commitments that don't bring us pure joy or move us forward is an important part of clearing the clutter in our lives. Learning how to say "No" in ways that are comfortable for us puts us back in control of our lives and enables us to focus on what we enjoy and do well, rather than continuing to over-promise and under-deliver.

~Lynne A. Edris, ACG

Lynne A. Edris, ACG, Life & ADHD Coach, CHADD Parent 2 Parent Trainer, ADD Coach for Dr. Kenny Handelman at Attention Difference Insiders www.CoachingADDvantages.com (717) 877-9853

ADHD and Organizational Systems

The best organizational system in the world is utterly useless if you can't use it! Give yourself some peace. There are many really good systems out there, yet they don't work for everyone. Your system doesn't need to work for anyone but you. Let go of the story that you "should" be able to make someone else's system work. Collect, glean, gather, and compile from all available resources to create something that works for you. You might find you were working too hard to make something fit that simply didn't.

~Ian King, Coach/Speaker

Ian King, Coach/Speaker specializing in ADHD and gifted adults, children, families, and entrepreneurs. Past President of ADHD Coaches Organization & ICF Chicago. www.KingSolutionsInc.com

Getting Back to Whole Foods

Here are 9 simple tips to get you out of the box and into the garden:

1. Live by this rule: If it doesn't rot or sprout, do without.
2. Eat protein, fats and complex carbs at every meal.
3. Be simple; introduce one new food at a time.
4. Stop buying boxed, bagged or canned foods that have more than five ingredients on the label.
5. Offer 'good for you' sweet foods like strawberries, cherries, sweet peas and sweet potatoes.
6. Add finely-chopped fruits to salads, stir pureed sweet peas into guacamole, and serve tiny vegetables with healthy dips.
7. Finely chop carrots, broccoli and green beans and mix into spaghetti sauce, taco meat, and hamburgers.
8. Make fruit muffins.
9. Be patient. Change takes time.

~Lynne Kenney, PsyD

Invite Dr. Kenney and The Parenting Team to give a brain-based parenting and educational skills teleseminar at your school or PTO. www.lynnekenney.com

Detailed Lists, Get Things Done

Instead of writing a "laundry" list of BIG tasks, write a "wash whites," "tumble dry whites," "fold whites," "put whites back in drawer/closet" list of small tasks. Do the same with "cleaning" (BIG task); instead, write "clean," "dust," "vacuum" (small tasks). Get the picture?

Small tasks = Less time-consuming!

Every time you cross out a task on the list, you'll feel energized. Turn it into a game to get it done faster!

Ask yourself this question: What do I want to do now? Pick the task you find most interesting, just do it, and then pick another one!

~Charlotte Hjorth, ADHD Coach

Charlotte Hjorth is the first Professional ADHD Coach in Denmark, initiator of the ADHD Awareness Week Denmark campaign in 2008, supervisor, writer, speaker, and educator www.adhd-coaching.dk

Free at Last!

When going off to college, high school seniors think – free at last!

That freedom works against the ADHD student. Unstructured college life is full of temptations like hanging out, partying, and sleeping it off.

Unstructured life hits ADHD students hard; they must build structures in order to thrive. Remember, just getting to class on time is struggle enough for the ADHD student.

When you arrive on campus, check out the disabilities center to see what support systems are provided.

If enough support is not available, fight for it! Meanwhile, look outside your campus for coaches and other experts to help.

~Abigail Wurf, M.Ed.

ADHD Coach Abigail Wurf, M.Ed My life experience/training makes me confident that together, we can make a positive difference in your life! www.abigailwurf.com www.awurf@verizon.net
(202) 244-2234

Change Two Letters and Expand Your World!

How many times each day, or maybe each hour, do you say or think the word "should?"

If you're like me, the answer would be, "Lots!"

You now have the opportunity to easily shift this habit.

You can actually change your thoughts by removing the letters "sh" from the word "should" and replacing them with the letter "c," thus creating the word "could."

This small change causes a huge shift in perspective by erasing the shame created by the word "should" and creating a whole new world of choice with the word "could!"

~Dee Doochin, MLAS

Dee Doochin, MLAS, Professional Certified Coach, Certified Mentor Coach, Senior Certified ADHD Coach, wife, mother, grandmother, great-grandmother with ADHD, adventurer, lover of life! www.addupcoach.com

"Don't let what you cannot do interfere with what you can do."

~John Wooden

Beat the Blues

Some of my favorite coaching clients are students. I love working with them as they discover more successful ways to manage their academic challenges. One of these strategies is simply to get them to use a planner. They start out the school year very enthusiastic, but often by winter break they are "bored." They stop entering due dates and start missing homework assignments. At the start of winter term, in order to restart their interest in a once-successful strategy, I present them with a "beat the winter blues" student kit. The new highlighters, pens and post-it notes for their planner renews their interest and has them back on track for success.

~Laurie Dupar, PMHNP, RN, PCC

Laurie Dupar, PMHNP, Certified ADHD Coach, specializes in helping you understand your brain, navigate the treatment maze, reduce your challenges and get things done! www.CoachingforADHD.com

Out the Door...On Time

You have no hope of being on time if you don't know how long it takes to get there.

Is it only 10 minutes? Or is it more like 25?

How long does it really take to get from your front door at home to your desk at work?

This is a word problem like you had in math class! If you drive 20 miles at 60 mph, it will take you about 20 minutes. If you drive 75 mph, you only save about 4 minutes! Does that really matter?

If you're regularly late when you start to get ready each morning, lay out your clothes the night before. Or shower faster!

~Kerch McConlogue, PCC, CPCC

Kerch McConlogue, PCC, CPCC, www.mapthefuture.com
(410) 929-3274

Prime the Pump to Feel The Love Again

Couples often say "I just don't feel in love anymore." So I ask, "Are you still doing what you did when you fell in love?" I usually get blank stares in response.

Did you know that when you do loving things for people, the action itself makes you feel love for them? When you stop doing those things, you no longer inspire those feelings. So, prime the pump. Make a list of what you did when you were courting, and do at least one thing every day. Then enjoy the love you feel and the response you receive.

~Cindy Lea, M.A.

Cindy Lea, MA, Psychotherapist, and ADD Coach & Speaker. Inspiring others by focusing on strengths and possibilities with warmth & humor. Minneapolis, MN (612) 965-3052
www.SucceedingWithADD.com Cindy@succeedingwithadd.com

Walk and Talk – Your Secret for Staying in Conversation

When relationships are strained, better communication can help both people feel heard, understood, and cared for. Most therapists will recommend improving communication by regularly talking and listening while sitting and looking at each other. The risk is that although the conversation may be important, the topic may be uninteresting, so staying engaged becomes harder. An alternative is to walk and talk. Walking adds kinesthetic and visual stimuli, which help with attention. It also decreases the pressure to "look at me when I'm talking to you," which can enhance listening. Try it, and see if it works for you.

~Dr. Roland Rotz, Ph.D.

Dr. Roland Rotz, Ph.D., and Coach Sarah D. Wright, M.S., A.C.T., internationally-known authors, speakers, and ADHD experts.
www.FidgetToFocus.com

Task Jumping? Stay on Track with a Random Thought Pad

It is common for ADHDers to complain about jumping from one unfinished task to another. Often this urge stems from the fear that whatever came to mind will be forgotten if not addressed immediately. The solution: a "Random Thought Pad" to jot down distracting thoughts as they pop up. Follow these simple steps toward greater productivity:

1. Commit out loud to completing a task or project.
2. When a distracting thought pops up – and it will – stop only for a moment to write it down.
3. Immediately return to the task. All of your great ideas and reminders will be waiting for you when you are done.

~Linda Richmand, Life Coach

Linda Richmand, Business, Career, and Life Coach specializing in adult AD/H/D. www.CoachRichmand.Com (914) 330-9103

Remain Vigilant

Many of my clients get a false sense of security once they make a few gains and abandon the strategies that got them there, thinking they don't need them anymore. They end up just where they started: stressed and in a world of chaos. It's important to realize that one of the hallmarks of ADHD is that you'll forget you have it. Structures and strategies are necessary to your wellbeing. Be vigilant in using strategies! Don't let down your guard!

~Nancy A Ratey, Ed.M., MCC

Nancy A. Ratey, Ed.M., MCC, is a Strategic Life Coach specializing in coaching professionals with ADHD. She is the author of *The Disorganized Mind*, www.NancyRatey.com

Supplements for Brain Health

Since our brain is made of fat, it is very important to have good fats included in our diet. These good fats help optimize dopamine, our focus neurotransmitters. To supplement, fish oil is best for children and adults since it is already in the EPA and DHA format that is needed for good communication of neurotransmitters. Flaxseed oil is a good food additive but it does not convert well for children since they do not have the proper enzymes yet for the breakdown to EPA and DHA. Amino acids used for focus are tyrosine and dl-phenylalanine. Testing for levels should be considered prior to implementing amino acids.

~Pam Machemehl Helmly, CN

Pam Machemehl Helmly, CN, is the Chief Executive Officer for Neurogistics, specializing in Neurotransmitter Testing and Amino Acid Therapy. www.neurogistics.com

Stop Interrupting Me!

In order to communicate more effectively, make sure that internal and external distractions are at a minimum. Internal distractions can be desiring to jump in and give advice, judging what the other person is saying, or letting your mind wander. External distractions can be the telephone, television, computer, pets, or other people. By limiting or eliminating each of these two forms of distractions, you will have more energy to focus on the task at hand: not only listening, but hearing as well.

~Laurie Moore Skillings, SCAC

Laurie Moore Skillings, Senior Certified ADHD Coach, specializes in working with teens that have a hard time with school. Laurie can be reached at laurie@addwithease.com.

Mothers First

Mothers, especially those whose children have ADHD or other difficulties, have a tendency to place others' needs ahead of their own. It would be wise to follow the recommendation of the flight attendants who advise passengers that if there is a loss of cabin pressure, parents should put the oxygen masks on themselves first and then on their children. When parents take care of themselves with a good diet, regular exercise and sufficient sleep, they have the wherewithal to deal with the challenges of raising children and fully enjoy its rewards. For more info go to: www.FocusForEffectiveness.com/blog.

~Roxanne Fouche, ADHD Coach

Roxanne Fouche, ADHD Coach and Consultant, specializes in working with individuals of all ages with ADHD/LD and related challenges. Roxanne@FocusForEffectiveness.com (858) 484-4749

Make a Planning System Work!

An effective planning system is a number one strategy for people with ADHD to better organize, prioritize and manage time. However, people with ADHD often find planning to be boring or cumbersome and have never found a system that works for them. Whether you prefer a smart phone, computer, or monthly/weekly/daily planners, these tips will help to make it effective:

1. Use it! Enter all deadlines, appointments, etc. Always!
2. Use one main planner…everything is entered into it.
3. At the beginning of a week, review that week's activities.
4. Check in with your "planner" each morning for that day's goals.
5. Check it again at the end of your day, moving unmet goals to where they can be accomplished.

~Laurie Dupar, PMHNP, RN, PCC

Laurie Dupar, Certified ADHD Coach www.CoachingforADHD.com

Improving Communication, Social Skills and Accommodations

Many people with ADHD are verbal processors . That is, they think out loud (talk out loud) when thinking about something or thinking about doing something. They do not always need or want a response. Make an agreement with people around you that when you are "verbally processing," they don't have to pay close attention nor respond unless you have specifically used their name. It takes practice, but it is worth it for everyone included.

~Marie Enback, ADHD Coach

Marie Enback is the first ADHD Coach in Sweden, initiator of ADHD Awareness Week Sweden, conference organizer, writer, speaker and educator. www.adhdcoaching.se
www.adhdawarenessweek.se www.lateralia.se

Finding Strengths

Whether at work, looking for a job, or in a relationship, knowing what your strengths are can help you a lot. I have my clients buy the book Strengths Finder 2.0 by Tom Rath and use the code in the back of the book to take the test to find their top 5 strengths. They can then use those strengths to set themselves apart from others in a good way to get a job, get a promotion or to help in finding a career. Many clients say they don't have strengths, only weaknesses, and this can also help build their confidence.

~Deb Bollom, PCC, ACG

Deb Bollom, PCC, ACG, works with entrepreneurs and adults who hate details and feel overwhelmed to discover their strengths and create ways to move forward.www.d5coaching.com (715) 386-6860

Personal Metaphors

People have a hard time seeing themselves and their needs objectively. That's why the AttentionB method utilizes personal metaphors. For example, I have a client who says he feels like an angry mountain gorilla most days.

By assigning an animal to his feelings, he now has a symbolic indicator of his emotions. I asked him what animal he would rather be. Let's say he wants to be a turtle, which is quiet and slow. He now has a clearer picture of his own needs: to slow down and have more quiet time. What animal do you want to be?

~Dr. Billi, Ph.D.

The AttentionB Method, Neuro-Cognitive Behavioral Therapy/Coaching www.AttentionB.com (855) Dr Billi

Accentuate the Positive of ADHD

1. Practice gratitude. Take time each day to acknowledge your blessings and what you are thankful for. They exist.
2. What's good about that? When the curve ball or unexpected happens, you have the power to choose your response and next move. How can you make the most of your strengths and create a better outcome?
3. Celebrate when you can! What fills your bucket? Keep a list handy of ways to celebrate and acknowledge your accomplishments. This can be extra time for yourself, a favorite activity, or something to purchase. Make it yours.

~Robin Nordmeyer, ADHD Coach

Robin Nordmeyer , ADHD Coaching Specialist
Robin@LifeAheadCoaching.com

What Worked for My Reluctant Reader and Writer

ADHDers learn when it's novel! The one-size-fits-all approach wasn't working to teach my child to read and write in school. What worked? Instant pudding, shaving cream, finger paints, and this huge roll of paper I taped to my kid's bedroom wall! We wrote on the kitchen counter with instant pudding, in the bath tub with shaving cream, and on her papered bedroom wall with finger paints: letters, spelling words, stories. The physical movement and sensory involvement made the language stick, freed my daughter from fears over neatness, spelling, and the "pencil," and most importantly built her confidence that translated into the classroom.

~Sandy Alletto Corbin, M.A., SCAC

Ms. Sandy Alletto Corbin, M.A., SCAC, Certified Senior ADHD Coach and Advocate working with families, teens and women. She can be reached at www.lifecoachsandyalletto.com

Get a Great Brain-Based Coach

A great ADHD coach:

- Doesn't ask you to "just try harder," but understands how brain differences affect your behavior and outcomes.
- Believes you have untapped potential and validates your reality.
- Helps develop your natural skills and talents rather than focusing only on problems.
- Looks for the greater truth hidden amid too many confusing thoughts at once.
- Listens with empathy, re-framing your negative self-talk into a neutral or supportive self image.
- Views you as capable, skillful, valuable and talented until you can see yourself that way.
- Helps you identify what is most important amid the buzz of too many thoughts or ideas at once.

~Glen Hogard, SCAC

Glen Hogard, SCAC, ACO Co-Founder. Serving students, academicians and creative entrepreneurs in the US and internationally via telephone since 1999 www.glenhogard.com www.worldADHD.com

Laundry Strategies for Clean Clothes

With ADHD, laundry can become a big problem for some people. Try doing laundry on the same day each week or making a habit of doing it at the same time of day. You can also outsource laundry to a local dry cleaner.

Have trouble remembering to put clothes into the dryer? Try one of the following:

- Carry a dryer sheet with you until you move the laundry to the dryer.
- Set TWO timers to help you remember.
- Put a note on the door into your house.
- Put a note on the microwave door.

~Laura Rolands, ADHD Coach

Laura Rolands is an Attention and ADHD Coach who helps students and adults pay attention and increase productivity. Connect with Laura at: www.MyAttentionCoach.com or www.Twitter.com/CoachforADHD

"If you run into a wall, don't turn around and give up. Figure out how to climb it, go through it, or work around it."

~Michael Jordan

Help for Clutter Bugs

This tip is for both children and adults and was a lifesaver in my family.

My ADHD son was very creative and treasured each of his masterpieces. Whether it was a drawing, toothpick sculpture or Lego creation, he simply couldn't bear to part with it. His room was closing in on him.

A wise and organized friend suggested we make a photo album dedicated to his art. My son enjoyed the process and was proud to have his masterpieces archived for all time.

'Things' have a way of cluttering our homes and our minds. Consider easing the pain of 'letting go' with an album celebrating those things you don't want to forget.

~Becky Wheeler, ADHD & Life Coach

Rebecca C. Wheeler, ADHD & Life Coach, New Focus Coaching, LLC, Alexandria, VA Structure * Skills * Strategy * Support bwheeler@newfocuscoach.com (703) 980-0809

With or Without?

After being on ADHD medications for awhile, many adults want to determine if they can as effectively manage their symtpoms without medication. As an ADHD Coach and Nurse Practitioner, I know it is important for people with ADHD to have confidence in whatever management system they are using, including medications. Keeping this in mind, ALWAYS first consult with your doctor. Only after medical consultation should you set some specific, objective parameters for yourself to gauge whether or not this new strategy is working. Ask yourself, "How will I know if I am managing my symptoms better without medications? And when will I know this?" Set an appointment date with your prescriber to help you re-asses your options

~Laurie Dupar, PMHNP, RN, PCC

Laurie Dupar, Nurse Practitioner & ADHD Coach, specializes in helping you understand your brain, navigate the treatment maze, reduce your challenges and get things done! www.CoachingforADHD.com Laurie@CoachingforADHD.com

Messages are All Around – Be Open

Having taken college courses over the years, I returned full-time, later in life. One day, while studying in Barnes & Noble, a man stopped and asked me what I was reading; although taken by surprise, and feeling a bit stressed and challenged, I truly welcomed the distraction, and told him what I was doing. The man looked at me and said, "Inch by inch, life is a cinch, yard by yard it's hard"... he smiled, walked away and we never met again. Thank you, my messenger - I earned my BA at age 45 after 23 years.

~Cindy Giardina, PCC

Cindy Giardina, Professional Certified Coach, specializing in adults and student with the talent of ADHD. Contact Coach Cindy: www.kaleidoscope-coaching.com cindy@kaleidoscope-coaching (973) 694-5077

Get Ready to Get Ready to Go!

Years ago, my girlfriend realized that I was rarely ready when it was time to leave the house. One day she gently said, "Rudy… it's time to get ready to get ready to go."

This simple request was an important lesson for me about that elusive step of 'getting ready' for transition to what's next, rather than waiting until the last minute.

Rudy, it's time to get ready (gather my keys, calendar, notes) to get ready to leave my office so I can arrive at the meeting on time. So, what are you getting ready to get ready for?

~Coach Rudy Rodriguez, LCSW

Coach Rudy Rodriguez, began working with ADHD in 1981 and was diagnosed with ADHD in 1983. He is the Founder of 'ADHD Center for Success'.

Tickler File

Can't find that email? Maybe it's in the Tickler File!

A tickler file is an upright accordion folder with pockets numbered 1-31 to help manage paper and information such as emails, mail, and meeting agendas requiring action.

An email arrives on the 1st of the month requiring you to complete a task by the 10th. Print the email. On the 8th of the month in your calendar, block time to complete the task. Put the letter "T" (for tickler) next to it. Put the email in the tickler file in the 8th pocket. Now the email is easy to find and your planner tells you where to find it.

~Joyce A. Kubik

Joyce Kubik, ADHD Coach www.bridgetosuccess.net

Memorize Boring Facts!

Children who have ADHD often struggle to memorize facts and definitions, especially when they find the topic boring or when it doesn't connect to anything they already know. Learning doesn't have to happen at a desk and in quiet concentration. Get them moving! Be creative and flexible.

- Have a catch; as you say the word, they say the answer.
- Spread flash cards out and play the game Concentration.
- With the cards spread out, have them throw a ball and whichever card it lands on, they must say the answer.
- Let them do jumping jacks or skip rope as you test them.

~Cindy Goldrich, Ed. M., ACAC

Cindy Goldrich, Ed. M., ACAC, Certified ADHD Parent Coach
www.PTScoaching.com Cindy@PTScoaching.com
(516) 802-0593 Coaching available in New York and Telephone.
Parent the Child YOU have!

At-Work Remedies for Managing Your Restlessness

Forgot your morning meds and now you are in a spin at school or work? Remember back before your treatment, when you fidgeted? That wasn't nervousness; it was defense against boredom, an attempt to keep your mind active and working. Your memory and your recall work better if your brain isn't bored. So deliberately do some "socially acceptable" fidgeting: wiggle your foot (quietly!) or play with your watchband, your bracelet, your necklace. Keep little "fidget beads" or a rubbing stone in your pocket or purse. Twirl your hair, touch your lips. And next time, keep some spare pills with you!

~John I. Bailey, Jr., MD

John I. Bailey, Jr., MD, Center for Attention & Learning, Mobile, AL
adddoc@bellsouth.net

Seeing Spots

Got piles everywhere? Want less of that? Read on, and I will share.

Things in a pile can have better spots by creating a new "home" for that one sort of thing and remembering to "KINDLY RETURN WITH CARE".

Too hard, you say? And how to start? You can find out right away.

Get a piece of paper Nice and big and cut it into circle shapes....

Label it "bills" or "transparent tape",

Place the spots where there would be piles on shelves, countertops or floors.

Now when you "see spots" you will know... you're more organized than you were before.

~Melissa R. Fahrney, M.A., CPC

Melissa Fahrney, M.A., CPC ADHD/Stress Management Coach for kids, college students & adults www.ADDHeartWorks.com www.facebook.com/addheartworks (888) 327-5727 "Don't stress out, master your mountain, with heart!"

Living with the EDGE

Many people with ADHD often find themselves STUCK. They are up against an EDGE of something and don't know what to do.

Whether that EDGE is a new job or relationship, a frustrating project, or just a funny feeling that holds them back, here's a quick, easy way to gain momentum and move forward:

E Explore the situation. Expand on what's working. Eliminate anything not working.

D Dream the ideal. Decide what you want to do. Delegate what don't want to do

G Gather information. Get into action GO!

E Experience the differences. Evaluate the results and then circle back and… EXPLORE again!

~Kricket Harrison, Speaker

Kricket Harrison, Professional Coach and Motivational Speaker, is an expert at maximizing creative potential and developing strategies for success based on individual learning styles. www.BrightOutsidetheBox.com

Exercising

Exercising can be an invaluable activity for taming the overactive mind. Although we have a garage full of equipment and I can certainly appreciate the convenience of exercising at home, you'll more likely find me in the gym. The gym offers multiple stimuli to allow my mind to wander unrestrained. It also has a quiet room, when that is my preference. I can switch machines every ten minutes or spend an hour on one piece. My mind's preference switches day to day; the gym allows me unlimited options in one location.

~Karen Peak, CPA

Karen Peak - not your typical certified public accountant - runs a successful tax and bookkeeping practice in Northern California, helping entrepreneurial clients from coast to coast. www.karenpeakcpa.com

The Backpack Battles

Homework can be frustrating when struggling with ADHD, especially after a long school day. Before tackling the backpack, try:

- Boosting brain power by eating a protein, carbohydrate, and good-fat snack beforehand.
- Making a to-do list with your child before tackling homework; break up assignments for them and add an estimated time frame for each assignment.
- Taking a break in between assignments or after 30 minutes as a reward and to reduce excess stimulation.
- Keeping phones and Internet away from work areas; let them use it during their break or after they are complete.

~Emily Roberts, MA, LPC

Emily Roberts, MA, LPC, is a psychotherapist who works with Neurogistics and helps parents balance their child's brain naturally. www.Neurogistics.com

What Have You Done for You Lately?

We all have to-do lists – the tasks we want to complete. How about keeping a "done list" of the tasks you have accomplished?

When you have lots to do, it helps to see that you are accomplishing plenty. Try keeping your done list where you keep your task lists. Or use www.IDoneThis.com to keep track. Simply reply to their daily email and they keep a calendar for you of your accomplishments.

Consider keeping track of tasks accomplished, in general, or specifically what you are doing for self-care.

~Kathy Peterson, ADHD Coach

Kathy Peterson, ADHD Coach since 1994, works with adults, primarily professionals, entrepreneurs, and people in corporate business and science; located in Arlington, MA; credentialed by ICF. www.petersoncoaching.com

Is This Hoarding?

Be careful not to believe everything you see on TV. Having a lot of stuff is not necessarily hoarding. People with ADHD are often overwhelmed with organizing their homes, and they also tend to be exuberant, intellectually curious people—two key contributors to clutter. If you have more stuff than you have room for, talk to a professional organizer with SPECIFIC experience in chronic disorganization. If you find it emotionally difficult to discard things, talk to a therapist with SPECIFIC experience in hoarding. And either way, remember that objects exist to serve you, not vice versa.

~Debbie Stanley, LLPC, NCC, CPO-CD

Debbie Stanley is a licensed mental health counselor specializing in chronic disorganization and hoarding, both of which often co-occur with ADHD. www.thoughtsinorder.com

Take a Walk in Your Child's Shoes

Have you ever thought what it would be like to go to work every day having to listen to criticism from your boss and your colleagues? Hearing that you are not working hard enough? Upon arrival at home, looking forward to some peace and quiet, you are faced with more demands and more criticism. You have not heard one positive word all day long! This is what some of your children experience daily. It is no wonder why these children feel like they are walking on eggshells, not knowing when and from whom the next negative comment will come from.

~Roya Kravetz, Life Coach

Roya Kravetz Life Coach and a parent instructor specializes in ADHD coaching and consulting with youth and adults with ADHD regarding ADHD and/or related challenges.

Perfecting Fidgeting – Tools for Staying Focused, Alert, and on Task

Fidgeting is NOT the same as multi-tasking (switching attention quickly from one task to another), which has a negative impact on performance. Instead, fidgeting is a mindless secondary activity that adds stimulation to any task, making it easier to remain focused and alert.

Fidgeting at its best helps you stay on task but doesn't bother the people around you. Clicking pens, drumming fingers, humming, or snapping gum are often no-nos. Wiggling toes and feet, doodling, using headphones, pacing, or simply standing up are usually great. Experiment to find out what works best for you in various settings.

~Sarah D. Wright, M.S., A.C.T.

Roland Rotz, Ph.D. and Coach Sarah D. Wright, M.S., A.C.T., internationally-known authors, speakers, and ADHD experts. www.FidgetToFocus.com

What to Ask When Choosing a Doctor

Choosing a doctor you trust when you/someone you love has ADHD is an important decision. Ask the following questions to help find the right one for you.

- "How long have you been working with ADHD? What percent of your practice is ADHD?" Experience counts.
- "How familiar are you with adult…adolescent…childhood ADHD?" Some doctors specialize.
- "How do you determine a diagnosis?" Thoroughness is key. Expect questions about medical history and wanting input from others.
- "How do you treat ADHD?" It's important that you agree on treatment options.
- "How do you work with clients who have ADHD?" Listen for such statements as: "Together we will..." or "I will work with you…"

There are no "right" answers. You want someone you feel comfortable with, someone who listens…is compassionate, experienced and professional.

~Laurie Dupar, PMHNP, RN, PCC

Laurie Dupar, Psychiatric Nurse Practitioner, ADHD Coach, www.CoachingforADHD.com

"The important thing is not being afraid to take a chance. Remember, the greatest failure is to not try. Once you find something you love to do, be the best at doing it."

~Debbi Fields

The Power of a Success List

When you're feeling down, these strategies will help you raise your self-esteem and remind you of what you have accomplished already and who you are!

Write down everything you have successfully completed, such as:

- Graduated
- Acted in a play
- Completed First Aid/CPR Certification...etc.

Just keep adding, and keep the list handy; you'll add to it often!

Next, write your "I ams":

- I am SMART
- I am in a play
- I am an actor
- I am certified in First Aid/CPR
- I am concerned, compassionate, helpful, etc.

Your first list describes WHAT YOU DO, and your "I AM" list is WHO YOU ARE!

Congratulations!

~Kathleen R. Marikar, ADHD Coach

Kathleen Marikar, ADHD Coach, Central, MA (978) 212-5855

Celebrate the Small Stuff!

What do you celebrate?

A new job, a fitness accomplishment, an acceptance to the college of choice. All of these are reasons to celebrate, but why do we wait for "big ticket items"?

What would your day be like if you celebrated getting grounded and making a choice by yourself? If you chose to quiet your gremlins, notice AND not judge? Try something new even if it didn't turn out 'perfect'?

Take the challenge!

Be on the lookout for the little things and celebrate them -- any way you want! Catch your student, teenager, husband and yourself and mindfully celebrate and acknowledge!

~Ana Isabel Sánchez, ADHD Coach

Mom. Wife. Attorney. Certified Coach with ADHD Training. Passion: Helping others take ownership of their lives and focus on their strengths to reach success.

How's All That Blame and Shame Working for You?

The key to a strength-based approach to managing ADD is in getting rid of blame and shame. When you are mired in the blame and shame of your ADD challenges, you are not approaching your struggles proactively and you are functioning from a place of weakness, not strength. Take out the blame, shame, and ensuing moral judgments from your own thoughts about your ADD, and you become able to use your tremendous problem-solving skills and wonderful out-of-the-box ADD thinking to come up with creative ways to address those challenges. Shifting our perspective toward our strengths improves our functioning and our fulfillment!

~Lynne Edris, ADHD Coach

Lynne Edris is a woman with ADD, Mom to an ADHD Teen, and a professional ADD Coach. "My life is like the ADD channel: All ADD, All the Time!"

10 Tips to Better Listening Skills

1. Become aware of your tendency to mentally roam.
2. When your mind wanders, mentally repeat what the person is saying.
3. Watch the person's mouth or eyes.
4. Ask questions; you'll become more engaged.
5. In a class or meeting? Bring fidgets or doodle.
6. Snap a rubber band on your wrist if you interrupt too much.
7. Don't be afraid to ask the person to repeat himself.
8. Pretend that you'll be tested on the information you're hearing.
9. Repeat (some!) of the words the speaker is saying so that it "sticks."
10. Eliminate distractions.

~Terry Matlen, MSW, ACSW

Terry Matlen, ACSW, a nationally-recognized authority specializing in women with ADHD, is the author of *Survival Tips for Women with ADHD* and founder of www.ADDconsults.com

The Power of Praise

It's always best to give more rewards and positive praise than negative comments or consequences. For most parents, the number of negative comments made to their children is far greater than the number of positive comments, and this is particularly true of kids with ADHD. Remember to catch them being good. Let them know specifically what they did well. Let other people know what they did well. Even though positive behavior may be expected or taken for granted in other children, praising and encouraging your child with ADHD is a surefire way to inspire them to show more positive behavior.

~Anonymous

Under Pressure? Breathe!

Do you get surprised and upset when you're caught off-guard by an unexpected question? Your anxiety and stress levels shoot sky high, like right away. You can't think clearly because your brain shuts down under this pressure. How do you manage the feeling of being blind-sided and confused? Does it feel like an attack?

Remember, you don't do anything wrong by taking your time to reply.

- Take a deep breath.
- Do you know the answer?
- Is it your responsibility to know the answer?
- Give yourself all the time you need to release the pressure and respond.

~Maureen Nolan

Coaching changes lives. Maureen coaches clients to discover attention solutions by uncovering their strengths, interests and values through creative conversations and exercises.

When Do You Plan Your Day?

Some people have trouble getting started if they decide in the moment what to start. Planning a day ahead will help. There is something about getting up with a plan already in place that takes the burden off your ADHD mind and keeps you out of overwhelm. Start planning at least a day ahead now. Once that routine is in place, stretch out your plan for a week in advance and then a month. Consider how far out to go, then discuss with your advisors to make a plan for your success.

~Robb Garrett, MA, MCC, ACT

Robb Garrett, MA, MCC, ACT, President of ADHD Coaches Organization www.adhdcoaches.org

Yes, It Hurts, But DO Your Homework!

- Determine if you have any assignments.
- Obtain understanding of the assignments.
- You are responsible for recording assignments.
- Operate the steps needed to do assignments.
- Use a checklist for materials needed for assignments.
- Reach home with assignments and materials.
- Have a special place and time to do homework assignments.
- Oversee your own assignments.
- Make sure assignments are as complete, accurate and neat as possible.
- Establish a special place for completed assignments.
- Wait! Bring completed assignments to school.
- Open your backpack.
- Return finished assignments to teacher on time.

Keep it up!

~Laurie Moore Skillings, SCAC

Laurie Moore Skillings, Senior Certified ADHD Coach, specializing in working with teens that have a hard time with school. Laurie can be reached at laurie@addwithease.com

Five Ways To Set School Success

- Know your child's strengths and challenges (including academic areas, focus, organization, transitioning, social skills, homework issues, working within time limits, etc.).
- Organize your files, including copies of school records, to prepare for effective meetings.
- Share what you know - and appropriate documents - with teachers at the beginning of the semester.
- Help your child with homework, as necessary, but let the teachers know the time spent and the type of assistance needed.
- Help your child develop self-advocacy skills so s/he understands what s/he needs and knows how to ask for it.

~Roxanne Fouche, ADHD Coach

Roxanne Fouche, ADHD Coach and Consultant, specializes in working with individuals of all ages with ADHD/LD and related challenges.
(858) 484-4749 www.FocusForEffectiveness.com/blog
Roxanne@RoxanneFouche.com

Brain Surfing & 31 Other Awesome Qualities of ADHD

I first heard the term "Brain Surfing" used by a client when she was describing the way it feels when her brain jumps from topic to topic or thought to thought. This unique ability to "brain surf" is frequently experienced by persons with ADHD when they are in the midst of something not very interesting. Although "brain surfing", can be distracting from the current subject at hand, it is an amazing ADHD brain's ability to keep itself occupied in the midst of a boring situation. Take advantage of your "brain surfing" quality and never be bored again!

Read about all 32 Amazing ADHD Qualities at www.CoachingforADHD.com

~Laurie Dupar, PMHNP, RN, PCC

Laurie Dupar, Certified ADHD Coach, specializes in helping you understand your brain, navigate the treatment maze, reduce your challenges and get things done! www.CoachingforADHD.com Laurie@CoachingforADHD.com

Imagining Your Way to Success

Need a little extra motivation? Get excited about the changes you can make by imagining the results as vividly as possible. What will achieving a particular change in your life feel like, look like, taste like, smell like, sound like?

You might visualize a diploma with your name written elegantly on it, a more organized or relaxed version of your life, or even a huge smile and hug from your mother.

Be as specific and detailed as possible as you imagine exactly how you will celebrate and enjoy the results of making that change. Now, go do it!

~Christina Fabrey, AAC

Christina Fabrey is a certified Life and ADHD Coach specializing in transition to college and college students. www.christinafabrey.com cfabrey@gmail.com (802) 345-2046

Start by Taking Stock

The process of peeling back the layers of your life can be as painful as it is positive. Putting your beliefs, assumptions, fears, values, and truths on the table, looking at them under a new light, and seeing how they stand up when challenged or questioned is no one's idea of a good time. But learning about your ADHD and how it is impacting your life is the key to taking advantage of your talents, mitigating your deficits, and managing your ADHD life in a non-ADHD world. Knowledge is power, and there is nothing more powerful than knowing yourself.

~Rori Boyce, AAC

Rori Boyce, AAC, ADHD Coach, Turning Leaf Life Coaching
www.turningleafcoaching.com rori@turningleafcoaching.com
(603) 731-9071

A Catalog of Interests

Kids with ADHD easily forget what they have around the house to keep them entertained. Out of sight, out of mind. Have your child inventory items or activities that they enjoy at home (example: Wii games, books, board games). Categorize them (which teaches them prioritization and organization). Don't overwhelm them by listing too many. Ask them to rank their interests. Choose only their top ten. Have them create a visual assemblage of these top interests by gluing symbols, pictures or cutouts onto poster board. They now have a visual chart to consult when they're bored, which organizes their interest-based activities into one convenient place.

~Dr. Billi, Ph.D.

The AttentionB Method, Parenting Tools for ADHD with Dr. Billi, Ph.D. Creative Parenting Strategies for ADHD that Get Results. Helping You Help Your Kids. www.AttentionB.com DrBilli@AttentionB.com
(855) Dr Billi

Put Your Tongue in My ear and I'll Follow You Anywhere

If that tongue in your ear was once hot and now has you cringing, it's better to say so than let him/her think you're recoiling from the whole experience. Does a very light touch feel like she's sucking your life energy? Or does his idea of massage feel like he's trying to rub your bones? Say something! And if you can't have that conversation in the moment, pick a time and do it later. If you think you can't look your "other" in the eye to say it, do it with your eyes closed, no matter where you are—well, except if you're driving, that is.

~Kerch McConlogue, PCC, CPCC

Kerch McConlogue, PCC, CPCC, works with adults in Baltimore and around the world who have ADHD. Find her on the web at www.mapthefuture.com

I'm In College! How Could I Have ADHD?

Like many adults, I didn't know that my poor auditory attention and poor working memory were attributable to ADHD!

Like many, I created compensatory strategies to succeed in college. Some refer to these strategies as 'hyper focus.' To listen to lectures, I wrote notes on everything the instructor said in class. I tape-recorded lectures and read a little each night to avoid becoming overwhelmed.

I found a buddy or two in each class to study with to help me remember better! I would study for half an hour, take a short break, then return to studying.

Doodling also helped me to listen.

~Lisa-Anne Ray-Byers

Speech-Language Pathologist, Author, Columnist and Education Advocate www.AskLisaAnne.com

Boundaries = Respect!

How often have you been told ADHD is a challenge of boundaries?

Have you ever wondered just what a boundary is?

Well, wonder no more. A boundary is a container that keeps you safe and allows you to be respectful of yourself and others!

A boundary is not a wall; it is loving arms around you that protect you and allow you to remain connected with yourself in spite of what else is going on around you.

It is a container that lovingly holds you together to keep you from disintegrating or splattering all over.

~Dee Doochin, MLAS

Dee Doochin, MLAS, Professional Certified Coach, Certified Mentor Coach, Senior Certified ADHD Coach, wife, mother, grandmother, great-grandmother with ADHD, adventurer, lover of life! www.addupcoach.com

Maintaining Self-Esteem

With the challenges that children with ADHD experience, it can be easy for them to begin to feel "less than" when compared to their peers. Maintaining self-esteem is critical to a child's success in school and later in life. Creating a home environment where people's differences are appreciated and their strengths are the area of focus helps to smooth those rough spots. Help your child realize that everyone has different things they do and don't do well. For instance, they may have difficulty with reading but do well in sports. Helping them see that everyone is different and focusing on their competencies will sustain their self-image and self-esteem to last a lifetime.

~Laurie Dupar, PMHNP, RN, PCC

Laurie Dupar, PMHNP, Certified ADHD Coach, specializes in helping you understand your brain, navigate the treatment maze, reduce your challenges and get things done! www.CoachingforADHD.com

Taking Time Out for Yourself!

There are some great tips and strategies on how to get organized or better manage your time. While those types of tips are important for people with ADD / ADHD, it's also very important to remember to take care of yourself. Self-care and taking time out for yourself is essential. This is not a luxury but is essential to living well with ADD / ADHD. First, make sure you give yourself permission to take a break and take time out. From there, practice taking breaks and time out on a regular basis.

~Tara McGillicuddy, SCAC

Tara McGillicuddy is a Senior Certified ADHD Coach and internationally-recognized ADHD Expert. Learn more about Tara and find her ADHD resources at www.youraddcoach.com

Motivation

I know what to do but can't make myself do it. Where is my motivation? For ADHD adults, motivation can be improved with these tips:

- If motivation is not coming from within, use things outside yourself to help. Enlist friends, set deadlines, hire help.
- Reward yourself (getting a snack, making a call, visiting a friend, taking a walk, stretching, going online).
- Remind yourself of your life goals/vision: Why are you doing this? Get a picture that reminds you of your life goals and post it.
- Catch yourself talking negatively to yourself and practice positive self-talk.

~Casey Dixon, M.S.Ed., CTACC

Casey Dixon, M.S.Ed., CTACC www.dixonlifecoaching.com

Manage ADHD Through Moving

After my diagnosis, I looked back at my past and found that the times that I was most successful where when running was a big part of my life. I embraced running and discovered that when my body moves, I am able to process information, solve problems and organize my thoughts, much the same way as when I take my medication. When I am in my stride, I feel like I am a thought machine that is powered by the movement of my body. ADHD has always represented a huge disconnection between what I wanted to accomplish, what I knew I had to accomplish and what my physical presence would ultimately allow me to do. Running merges these three things and makes me feel whole. I call these elements "thought, sweat & desire".

~Robert M. Tudisco, Esq.

Robert M. Tudisco, Esq., attorney, writer, ADHD adult and Executive Director of the Edge Foundation, a nonprofit that provides coaching support for students with ADHD www.edgefoundation.org

Portable Sorting

Arrange several small adjustable-height tables ($20 each) in a circle around you to sort big messes (especially piles of paper). If you get interrupted (and you WILL get interrupted), you can move them to a protected space in another room, then come back to sorting later. No one can "mess" with your mess.

~Linda Roggli, PCC/CLC

Linda Roggli, PCC/CLC Professional Certified Coach, Author of *"Confessions of an ADDiva: midlife in the non-linear lane"* http://confessionsofanaddiva.net

Help Your ADD Employee and You!

- Work together to create goals that are realistic, attainable and manageable; having defined goals will ease frustration and facilitate success.
- Don't overwhelm your employee with too many tasks/assignments at the first meeting; co-creating a game plan will produce great results.
- Create structure and ongoing accountability; this will turn great intentions into action.
- Be accessible; minimize the guesswork.
- Work in small spurts rather than long hauls.
- Recognize strengths and give support around weaknesses; the result will be steady job performance.
- Maintain a sense of humor and don't let them drive you nuts.

~Nancy Snell, CEC, PCC

Nancy Snell, CEC, PCC, NYC-Professional certified coach/consultant specializing in business/adult ADHD, and information overload solutions. Her bottom line is success with sanity. www.nancysnell.com (212) 517-6488

Finding and Keeping Friends

Finding and keeping friends can be hard for people with ADHD for many reasons. Some of these include: a tendency to interrupt when others are speaking; lack of follow-up or follow-through; constantly being late; inability to provide undivided attention to another person; and the existence of co-morbidities like depression or OCD. To meet other people, really push yourself to get involved with activities that play to your strengths. If after you get to know somebody, a problem arises, apologize, explain and together seek compromises that play to your assets, not your weaknesses. One example is have your friend call to remind you when to leave for an activity together.

~Abigail Wurf, M.Ed.

ADHD Coach Abigail Wurf, M.Ed. My life experience/training make me confident that together, we can make a positive difference in your life! www.abigailwurf.com awurf@verizon.net (202) 244-2234

Storing Things

Store things where you think they belong and where you will look for them. There's no right or wrong place as long as it works for you. Trust your instincts and know your habits.

Carrie Greene, Coach

Carrie Greene, speaker, trainer, coach and author of *Chaos to Cash*. She helps entrepreneurs cut through the chaos to make decisions, stop spinning and make more money. http://www.CarrieThru.com

Beware the "One More Quick Thing" Trap

Have you ever ended up late because you told yourself, "I'll just do one more quick thing before I go"? Your brain tricked you! When you take the focus from a pending time point, your brain kicks into overdrive, reminding you of things you need to do. Of course, it makes sense to want to squeeze them in while you're focused, but giving in to that temptation will cause you to be late. So, start with a list of what you want to accomplish with a red line after the last item. When more things pop into your mind, jot them on your list below the red line. Look at your list. Anything below that red line will make you late. Now you can see and make your choice.

~Barbara Luther, MCC

Barbara Luther, Master ADHD Certified Coach, www.WindBeneathYourWings.com President, Professional Association of ADHD Coaches, www.PAACCoaches.org Director of Training, ADD Coach Academy, www.addca.com www.SoaringCoachesCircle.com St. Louis, MO (573) 340-3559

Planned Spontaneity?

You're naturally spontaneous. Your partner may not be. While you think spontaneity is romantic, don't assume it is true for them.

You see spontaneity as exciting and engaging; your partner may see it as unplanned and thoughtless. You enjoy following an impulse to free your mind; your partner may see that impulse as a distraction from "what needs to be done."

So, when you're feeling spontaneous and want to do something romantic, use that energy to PLAN a romantic evening. For example, plan a nice dinner and be spontaneous by surprising her with flowers or an after-dinner stroll to her favorite cafe for dessert and coffee.

You can still be spontaneous – just plan for it and it won't go to waste!

~David Sloan

David Sloan, 31 yrs old, recently diagnosed with ADD
Columbia, SC

" The jump is so frightening between where I am and where I want to be. Because of all I may become, I will close my eyes and leap."

~Mary Anne Radmacher

Stuck in the ADD Quicksand Again!

When we ADDers are struggling to follow through, we are often stuck in a state of overwhelm that feels like quicksand. No amount of guilt or self-flagellation will help us move forward. Often, we find ourselves stuck when what we're trying to do is too big, too boring, or not well-defined. Next time, ask yourself what it is about what you're NOT doing that is holding you back. Too big? Break it down into single action steps you can take. Not well-defined? Give it a process/steps. Too boring? Make it more fun/interesting. Keep it simple, and pull yourself forward!

~Lynne Edris, ADD Coach

Lynne Edris is a woman with ADD, Mom to an ADHD Teen, and a professional ADD Coach. "My life is like the ADD channel: All ADD, All the Time!"

Human Beings "Doing"

As a trained Life Coach, I have come to appreciate the "being" part of living, such as the need I have for peace and solemnity in my life. It's refreshing to give myself permission to take a break, breathe deeply and enjoy the moment. I highly recommend it! I also know that a great deal of my personal satisfaction in life comes from "doing": keeping busy, moving my body, using my mind, creating, producing, "getting things done." Without both I feel unbalanced, unsettled. It's important to not forget to "be" a human being, but I also think that with the minds, bodies and hearts we have been blessed with, we also need to honor our need to "do." What is your balance?

~Laurie Dupar, PMHNP, RN, PCC

Laurie Dupar, PMHNP, Certified ADHD Coach, specializes in helping you understand your brain, navigate the treatment maze, reduce your challenges and get things done! www.CoachingforADHD.com

Embracing ADHD

There is no doubt our world is changing rapidly and the amount of information we need to process is expanding exponentially. It is possible that ADHD is a functional brain adaptation that allows people to multi-task, adapt rapidly to changing information, and creatively problem solve. Some of the most successful and brilliant minds of our time have had attention deficit. Learning to cope with it and work around its limitations is a little bit like riding a stallion. If you can harness the gifts and reign in the obstacles, you can truly fly.

~Dr. Susan Wilder, M.D.

Dr. Susan Wilder, CEO of LifeScape Medical Associates and LifeScape Premier, is an expert in nutritional testing and interventions for mood/attention problems in adults and children. www.lifescapepremier.com (480) 860-5269

The First Step

For those with ADHD, awareness is the gift from which all other great things come. It breaks the pattern, reveals the next opportunity, and provides a nudge or neon sign to show you the way. Whether it settles over you, allowing outdated behaviors and beliefs to fall away or slides into place like the last puzzle piece, becoming aware of all the things we are and all the things we aren't is the first step on the road to acceptance. It is this step that empowers you to take control of your life and consciously choose each step that follows.

~Rori Boyce, ADHD Coach

Rori Boyce, ADHD Coach, Turning Leaf Life Coaching, Alton Bay, NH
www.turningleafcoaching.com

Repeat and Then Answer the Question

My arguments with my significant other happened from responding to what I thought was being said, instead of what was actually being said. Following is what I did, but it takes practice. I explained to my partner HOW I needed to argue. I said I would repeat what s/he was saying to me first, to make sure I understood, and then I would need to take time to respond. Oftentimes, I was bombarded and pressured into responding, which only shut me down or made me emotional, and then nothing was accomplished. This worked.

~Sandy Alletto Corbin, M.A., SCAC

Ms. Sandy Alletto Corbin, M.A., SCAC, Certified Senior ADHD Coach and Advocate working with families, teens and women. She can be reached at http://www.lifecoachsandyalletto.com

Taking Charge of Your Time?

With ADHD, often there is a lack of time awareness. This lack of time awareness can allow you to make commitments that you do not want to make or that you will find difficult to keep. Create a default statement that you train yourself to make automatically whenever someone asks for you to volunteer, commit to a deadline, or otherwise commit your time and energy. That might be, "Let me check my calendar and other commitments and get back to you on the next working day."

~Robb Garrett, MA, MCC, ACT

Robb Garrett, MA, MCC, ACT, President of ADHD Coaches Organization www.adhdcoaches.org

Succeed Based on Who YOU Are

I've given up trying to do things the way I think I should or wish I could. Instead, I've found that by accepting who I am and embracing how I work best, I have more fun, I am happier and I get more done!

Popeye said it best, "I yam who I yam...". Being self-aware is good. Being self-critical only feeds overwhelm and self-doubt.

The right way of doing something is often the way that gets it done: *your* way, however unorthodox. Have fun using your creative brain to create unique strategies that work for YOU!

~Susan Lasky, ADHD Strategist

Susan Lasky is a Master ADHD Strategist and Productivity & Organization Coach, helping adults and older students to get things done and enjoy life! www.SusanLasky.com Susan@SusanLasky.com (914) 373-4787

Speed Cleaning with the Kitchen Timer

It doesn't take long before an ADD household gets messy. Plan time mid-day to put things back together in your home. Working room to room, set the kitchen timer for five minutes and tidy up one room. When the timer goes off, scoop up items that don't belong and place them in the kitchen. Reset the timer and move to the next room, taking what's appropriate for that room with you. Continue this process for the main floor, and additional floors if time permits. Remember to involve the kids when you can!

~Robin Nordmeyer, ADHD Coach

Robin Nordmeyer, ADHD Coach www.LifeAheadCoaching

When Parent and Child Have ADHD

When a parent shares a similar experience with their child, it is natural to identify and empathize with their child's challenges. Although empathy is important, balance and boundaries are key. Try these:

- Don't let your similarities cloud your responsibility or the need to set limits and boundaries for your child. Without boundaries or limits, the parent and child with ADHD tend to clash more.
- The ideal situation is to try to keep a balance, as hard as it can be. Parents can make it a priority to address their own difficulties first with such challenges as impulsivity or impatience so they can more effectively help their child.

~Roya Kravetz

Roya Kravetz, Life Coach, ADHD Coach and Consultant, and Parent Instructor, specializes in ADHD coaching and/or related challenges.
roya@adhdsuccesscoaching.com

The 123s

Train yourself to remember things in threes. Then all you have to remember is to ask yourself, "Right now, what three things do I need to remember?" Before leaving the house, they might be: remember keys, phone, wallet. Before leaving a classroom, they might be: hand in homework, confirm new assignment, put everything in backpack. When arriving home, they might be: hang up jacket, sort mail, walk dog. Once you get the hang of it, you'll use the 123s for everything!

~Sarah D. Wright, M.S., A.C.T.

Sarah D. Wright, M.S., A.C.T., internationally-known ADHD coach, speaker, author, expert, and founding Board Member of the ADHD Coaches Organization. Contact her at Sarah@FocusForEffectiveness.com

Delegating is not Dumping

One of the worst ways to use your amazing ADHD brain is to try and make your self do something it is not interested in. It doesn't mean that the task/job is not important, but when ADDers are not inherently interested, it will probably not get done. Instead, try creating a team around you who are enthusiastic about providing you support. Such members of your team might include:

- A teen to file paperwork, make copies, run errands, mow, weed, etc.
- A housekeeper
- A bookkeeper
- A laundry service
- A virtual assistant

Whenever we focus on doing those things we are uniquely suited for, everybody benefits!

~Laurie Dupar, PMHNP, RN, PCC

Laurie Dupar, Certified ADHD Coach, www.CoachingforADHD.com

Move It or Lose It! 5 Tips for Tactile/Kinesthetic/Haptic Learners

Tactile/Kinesthetic/Haptic learners learn best through moving, doing and touching. Here are a few tips to help you take advantage of your unique learning style:

Tip # 1: Chew gum to help stay focused.

Tip # 2: Lie on your back or stomach when studying. Feel free to kick your feet.

Tip # 3: Break it up. Study in short blocks of time. Include frequent breaks.

Tip # 4: Use flash cards. Review flash cards on a regular basis.

Tip # 5: Doodle. It helps with attention. Also, studies have shown that doodlers have increased retention.

~Laurie Moore Skillings, SCAC

Laurie Moore Skillings, Senior Certified ADHD Coach, specializes in working with teens that have a hard time with school. Laurie can be reached at laurie@addwithease.com

Visual Inspiration at Work

"Ah, if only you could dance all that you've just said, then I'd understand."

My favorite quote from Zorba the Greek hangs in my office and holds special meaning for me. So does a statue of Albert Einstein. A cartoon figure saying, "Genius at Work" sits above my desk.

Inspirational postcards line my bulletin board.

If I start to get sidetracked, there are visual and meaningful reminders in all four corners of my office to work smart using my own unique methods.

Identify what quotes or clippings inspire you to work at your peak potential. Display them prominently in your workspace.

~Dr. Billi, PhD.

The AttentionB Method, Expressive Arts Therapy for ADHD www.AttentionB.com (855) DrBilli

Staying Focused During Meetings

As an executive with ADHD, I attend a lot of meetings. I have found that taking a lot of notes in meetings keeps me focused on the conversation and helps me to remember later on what was discussed. For simplicity, I use a spiral notebook and date and title each page. I use different symbols in front of each note to highlight important parts. If an action item is assigned, I write an A in front of it and then circle it with a highlighter. After the meeting, I transfer the actions to my action item list. When a notebook is full, I put the start and end date on the cover to keep for later reference.

~Anonymous

Morning Routines to Beat the Rush

Are mornings a struggle? Does ADHD leave you rushing? Routines help adults with ADHD manage their mornings and beat the rush. Follow these five steps to establish your morning routine:

- Track how much time you spend on various tasks (brushing teeth, showering, eating, getting dressed, etc.) in the morning.
- Review the order of your tasks and how much time you spend on them.
- Decide which task order is most efficient for you.
- Set a goal for how much time you will spend on each task.
- Write or type your routine and post it.

Review and celebrate your successes each week.

~Laura Rolands, ADHD Coach

Laura Rolands is an Attention and ADHD Coach who helps students and adults pay attention and increase productivity. Connect with Laura at www.MyAttentionCoach.com or www.Twitter.com/CoachforADHD

Timers: Your Best Friend

Keeping track of time is often difficult for people with ADHD. To help, count-down and count-up timers are useful to:

- See how long certain tasks take to help with future planning.
- Visualize the allotted amount of time you set aside to work. (Time Timers© are great for this!)
- Let you know that it's time to take a break after X minutes of work.
- Get back to work from a timed break. (Key!)
- Set a limited period of time to do something especially onerous.
- Race the clock to see how much can get done in a certain amount of time.

~Roxanne Fouche

Roxanne Fouche, ADHD Coach and Consultant, specializes in working with individuals of all ages with ADHD/LD and related challenges. Roxanne@RoxanneFouche.com (858) 484-4749

Too Much Stuff—Inside and Out?

Physical clutter begets mental clutter. One of the first things I check into with my clients is what their physical space is like. For those of us with ADD, having too much "stuff" around us exacerbates the feeling of having too much "stuff" inside our heads. When we simplify our lives by clearing our physical spaces, we feel more able to focus. Where to start? Pick one place in your home/office that would make you feel more clear and in control. Now pick one part/surface of that place and start chipping away there; just 10-15 minutes a few times a day can make a big difference over time.

~Lynne A. Edris, ACG

Lynne A. Edris, ACG, Life & ADHD Coach, CHADD Parent 2 Parent Trainer, ADD Coach for Dr. Kenny Handelman at Attention Difference Insiders www.CoachingADDvantages.com (717) 877-9853

Be Gentle

Many with ADHD tendencies can have a belief that they must force their way through things in order get them done. This can work in the short term; however, it is simply not sustainable in the long term. What is called for is that we find our way to be gentle with ourselves while creating action, which may be no easy task! Most of us would never intentionally cause pain or be harsh or critical towards someone we care about, so why would it be acceptable for us to be so negative with ourselves?

~Ian King, ADHD Coach

Ian King, Coach/Speaker specializing in ADHD and gifted adults, children, families, and entrepreneurs. Past President of ADHD Coaches Organization & ICF Chicago. www.KingSolutionsInc.com

Take Time to Schedule

Many of us overestimate what we can do and underestimate the amount of time each task will take. Spend 5-10 minutes at the start of the day listing the specific tasks to be done that day. Next, assign a priority to each item. Lastly, with a different color pen, realistically estimate how much time that task will take you to complete. Over time, you will get a better idea of what you can do in a day, and you can use that to feel accomplished at the end of the day looking back on what you have done.

~Karen Peak, CPA

Karen Peak - not your typical certified public accountant - runs a successful tax and bookkeeping practice in Northern California, helping entrepreneurial clients from coast to coast. www.karenpeakcpa.com

The Feelings of ADHD

Management/treatment of ADHD is mostly focused on outward symptoms such as hyperactivity, distractibility or impulsivity. Less acknowledged are the common inner feelings/experiences of being diagnosed with ADHD, such as:

- Anger of not knowing sooner
- Grief for what "might have been"
- Isolation
- Shame
- Hope that this can be "fixed"
- Overwhelm
- Relief to know what "it is"
- Shock or denial that it's ADHD
- Sadness

Whether you are seven or seventy, the most important thing for persons with ADHD who might be experiencing these common feelings is to talk about them with someone you trust, such as your doctor, therapist, ADHD Coach, pastor, etc.

~Laurie Dupar, PMHNP, RN, PCC

Laurie Dupar, Nurse Practitioner and ADHD Coach www.CoachingforADHD.com

7 Things Adults with ADHD Want Their Partners to Know

We now know ADHD is not just a childhood disorder and symptoms frequently have a negative impact on relationships for adults. If you are in a relationship with someone who has ADHD, here are some things they would like you to know:

1. I have ADHD. I can't get rid of it. I am trying to manage it.
2. Remember to enjoy my uniqueness.
3. Don't forget about my positive qualities that attracted you to me in the first place.
4. ADHD is not an excuse, it is an explanation.
5. Even though it may not always seem like it, I do care, I am interested, I want to hear what you are saying and I don't want to hurt you.
6. I am trying. My brain makes it difficult, so please be patient.
7. When you take time to learn about ADHD, I feel hopeful.

~Anonymous

"Our greatest weakness lies in giving up. The most certain way to succeed is always to try just one more time."

~ Thomas A. Edison

Want to find out more about ADHD?

Visit Laurie Dupar at:

www.CoachingforADHD.com

www.facebook.com/CoachingforADHD

or email:

Laurie@CoachingforADHD.com

Share your own personal ADHD success tip:

We want to hear from you! Let us in on your personal favorite ADHD strategy, or tell me about your success story! I would love to hear from you! Please email me at: Laurie@ADHDAwarnessBookProject.com.

I look forward to hearing from you!!

~Laurie Dupar, Editor,
365 ways to succeed with ADHD

Made in the USA
Lexington, KY
11 October 2011